W9-CBN-477

Just Because You're on a Roll... Doesn't Mean You're Going Downhill

Just Because You're on a Roll ... Doesn't Mean You're Going Downhill

ROBERT A. SCHULLER

Fleming H. Revell Company
Old Tappan, New Jersey

Unless otherwise identified, Scripture quotations in this book are taken from The New King James Version. Copyright © 1979, 1980, 1982 Thomas Nelson, Inc., Publishers.

Scripture quotations identified NIV are from the Holy Bible, New International Version, copyright © 1973, 1978, 1984 International Bible Society. Used by permission of Zondervan Bible Publishers.

Scripture verses marked TLB are taken from The Living Bible, Copyright © 1971 by Tyndale House Publishers, Wheaton, Ill. Used by permission.

Scripture quotes identified AT are the author's translation.

Scripture quotation identified PHILLIPS is from *Letters to Young Churches* by J. B. Phillips. Copyright © 1947, 1957 by Macmillan Publishing Co., Inc., renewed 1975 by J. B. Phillips. Used by permission.

"High Flight" by John Gillespie Magee, Jr., is used by special permission from the International Herald Tribune, Paris, France.

Library of Congress Cataloging-in-Publication Data

Schuller, Robert A.
    Just because you're on a roll doesn't mean you're going downhill / Robert A. Schuller.
        p. cm.
    Includes bibliographical references.
    ISBN 0-8007-1643-4
    1. Success—Religious aspects—Christianity. 2. Christian life-—Reformed authors. I. Title.
BV4598.3.S37   1990
248.4—dc20   90-44137
                                                                  CIP

All rights reserved. No part of this publication may be reproduced, stored in a retrieval system, or transmitted in any form or by any means—electronic, mechanical, photocopy, recording, or any other—except for brief quotations in printed reviews, without the prior permission of the publisher.

Copyright © 1990 by Robert A. Schuller
Published by the Fleming H. Revell Company
Old Tappan, New Jersey 07675
Printed in the United States of America

Stella DeHaan is a woman who has succeeded in living. She has experienced life's greatest joys. God has blessed her. He has given her the strength and the ability to raise seven children, twenty-eight grandchildren, and fifty-two great-grandchildren. She is my mother's mother. On August 8, 1990, we celebrated her ninetieth birthday. She is an example of how God works and so I dedicate the following pages to her, my grandmother.

Contents

Introduction—
There's Got to Be
More to Life Than
This!

Have you ever been "on a roll"? Many people I meet associate being on a roll with success, well-being, and everything going well. Others, however, tell me, "On a roll? I'm on a roll all right—straight downhill."

As I counsel with people in my office or at lunch, all the familiar phrases pour out:

"Everything seems to be going wrong for me."

"All I have is problems, hassles ... I keep making mistakes."

"I'm in some sort of rut. How long is this going to last?"

"There's got to be more to life than *this!*"

Sometimes the hassles and problems are serious—failing marriages, a wandering mate, a lost job, not enough money to cover all the bills, or a teenager on drugs. In other cases, problems are more the run-of-the-mill variety: the boss is cranky again, Jimmy's report card is dotted with *D*'s and *U*'s, the car transmission is making odd sounds, the neighbor is irate because the children trampled his flower beds.

Whatever the downhill slide includes, it always seems to bring problems in bunches. It's the familiar "one thing after another" syndrome, and we can easily get caught right in the middle of it. I have been in a few of them myself! But we all know what it's like . . . sometimes we're on a roll upward and sometimes we're on a roll down. The key is to be able to recognize when we are on that negative downward slide and what we can do to get on a roll upward toward that illusive goal called *success*.

Success is a very subjective concept. Some people define success as "making it"—especially financially or career-wise. But I believe the best definition I've ever heard is simply this:

SUCCESS: THE PROGRESSIVE REALIZATION OF WORTHWHILE GOALS

Success is not a destination, but a progressive life-style and way of living. And I believe it is perfectly legitimate to seek success because success is God's purpose for us. Jesus said that He wanted us to have life and have it more abundantly.[1] What better description of success could we have than that?

When our first purpose is to glorify God, we can set worthwhile goals, and as we progressively realize those worthwhile goals, we reach our highest potential as individuals. That is what the abundant life is all about.

The more I work with people and their problems, the more I see a pattern of negative downward cycles and positive success cycles in several major areas of life. I am thinking particularly of the Spiritual, Emotional, Mental, and Physical areas, as well as Family, Friends, and Finances.

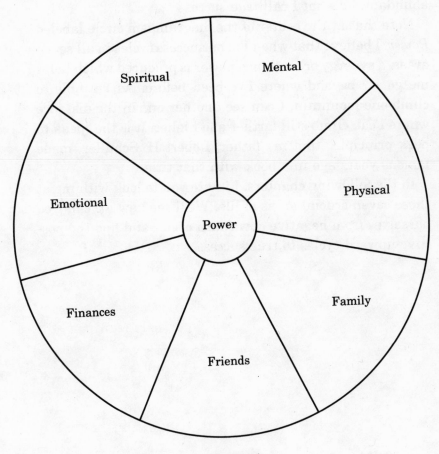

Figure 1

Figure 1 illustrates these areas. In each area, I have discovered factors involved in a negative downward cycle that produce frustration and feelings of continual failure. By contrast, I've also identified factors that contribute to a positive upward cycle for each area, producing the life more abundant, or what I call true success.

Note that at the center of the diagram is a circle labeled *Power*. I believe that when I'm on success cycles in all seven areas, a synergy or combined power is produced which helps me go far beyond where I've been before. As I'm able to climb one mountain, I can see another one in the distance where I can climb still farther and higher. It is the "peak to peek principle" that my father, Robert H. Schuller, made famous years ago in a book with that title.

In the following chapters, I invite you to look with me at these seven crucial areas of life. We'll see how we can free ourselves from negative downward cycles and find the positive upward cycles to true success.

Just Because You're on a Roll... Doesn't Mean You're Going Downhill

*L*ife
is
not
a
sprint
but
a
marathon.

———————◆———————

Chapter 1
Faith Gets the Wheels Turning

"I'm a basket case . . . it's as if I'm on autopilot, making mistake after mistake. I have the best of intentions but it never works out. I need to do something different. I need to *be* different. Something has to change!"

In the privacy of my office, Gay poured out her story, which had begun when she was a child growing up in a dysfunctional, alcoholic home. Practically all of her adult life had been one long, negative downward cycle. She'd been through failed marriages and the trials of being a single parent to her two children, and was blaming herself for everything that had gone wrong. She had found it necessary to move her children from school to school, and they had had trouble at times with their studies and adjusting to all the changes.

At one point, Gay lost her father and her job within the same two-week period. She couldn't function at work under normal stress conditions, and she didn't know how she could face an upcoming unavoidable surgery. She took tranquilizers almost daily, was crying constantly, and often found herself "barking at people."

As Gay described her troubles, I decided that I had never heard a more dramatic description of a negative downward cycle from anyone.

Without Faith You Are Programmed to Fail

Some downward cycles can last a few days or a few months. Gay's had lasted for many years. She realized she was in danger of having it last for life, and we were practically her "last hope."

Any downward cycle almost always begins with a failure—a mistake or goof of some kind. Usually it's your own failure, but sometimes the failure of others can deeply affect you because you take responsibility and blame. I talk to many parents who find themselves in a negative downward cycle because of the way their children are behaving (or misbehaving, to be more accurate).

In Gay's case, however, her parents had made the mistakes and she had paid the price by repeating the same cycle of failure over again. She had never become an alcoholic, but she had always managed to make bad choices in relationships and had suffered one disappointment after another.

Figure 2 illustrates the kind of downward cycle that had trapped Gay for so many years. From "I failed," it is natural enough to move to "I can't." Failure usually attacks our feelings of self-worth, and when we lack healthy self-esteem our faith melts away along with our drive and motivation. We begin to doubt that we could possibly succeed, especially in the area where we just failed.

As the downward cycle continues, we move from "I can't"

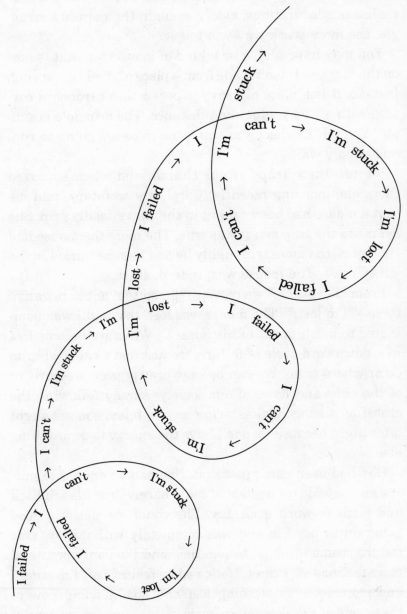

Figure 2: The Negative Downward Cycle to Spiritual Failure

to "I'm stuck." We start believing that we can't accomplish much of anything in life, that we can't reach our goals or realize our aspirations. Oddly enough, the more we struggle, the more stuck we seem to get.

You may have seen a new kind of mousetrap that is now on the market. It isn't made from a piece of steel on a spring. Instead, it is a piece of heavy paper or thin cardboard covered with a sticky, gluelike substance. The principle is simple: You put it where you think the mice are going to run, and simply wait.

We use these traps at our church, and when I arrived there one morning recently, Carol, my secretary, told me that a mouse had been caught in the trap's deadly grip. She led me to the trap and it was true. The more the mouse had struggled, the more thoroughly he had become buried in the sticky mess. The mouse was, indeed, stuck.

From "I'm stuck," we move to the bottom of the negative cycle—"I'm lost." (The mouse was lost, too, and I was nominated to put him out of his misery.) When we become lost in a downward cycle of failure, we just don't know what to do or where to go. We can be easy prey of peer pressure, or of the ebbs and flows of our society, simply following the crowd or sitting home staring at the television set night after night because we don't have the energy to do anything else.

Gay had been doing just that. She had no energy to pursue any outside interests and could barely drag herself back and forth to work each day. She could see nothing good going on in her life and was completely without joy. One failure seemed to lead to another, and that only produced more feelings of "I can't," followed by feelings of "I'm stuck" and more feelings of being lost and not knowing how to break out of her downward cycle.

"I'll bet you're feeling that life is against you," I observed as Gay paused for breath.

"Yes, I have to admit that I am. So where do I go from here?"

The First Step to "How Can I?"

"You've got to begin by having faith," I told her.

Gay's eyebrows arched a bit, and she looked at me as if to say, *Yes, that sounds like something my pastor would tell me—but what do I do? I'm almost all out of faith.*

"I realize that might sound a bit simplistic," I went on, "but I understand how you feel. I've been there myself, and it has always helped me to remember that we need only a tiny mustard seed of faith to get the wheels turning toward a positive cycle of success."

Gay was so low on that first day she came to see me that she left my office with only the tiniest amount of faith, but what she called "a lot of hope." She left hoping to have faith—hoping to believe. That was her first tiny step from saying, "I can't," to beginning to ask herself, "How can I?" With that simple decision, the impossible started to turn into the possible—even for her.

Gay told me later, "Learning that I didn't need to have a lot of faith opened the door for me and I felt there was hope. I realized all I needed to do was hope and have the desire and then I would be okay."

Gay didn't call me back a couple of days later to tell me that she had found some kind of instant solution. In fact, things had to get a little worse before they began to get better at all. But slowly, ever so slowly, over the next few months she started to turn the corner. I kept encouraging Gay to be patient, telling her that it didn't matter if things were going slowly. The point was that her life was changing for the good. I kept reminding her that life is not a sprint but a marathon, and once you get on a positive upward cycle, you can be productive for many, many years.

"I've decided I'm just not going to let it all happen again," she told me one day as we talked. "I'm going to do the things that will create a positive new life. Even if I just go through the motions—maybe something will rub off—something will work."

Once Gay took that first step from "I can't" to "How can I?" her success cycle started to roll, slowly at first, and then it began picking up momentum (*see* Figure 3). I like to put this particular cycle in the form of a little rhyme:

> *How turns into Now,*
> *Now turns into Wow,*
> *Wow turns into Pow,*
> *Pow turns into How!*

I have seen this success cycle work again and again in my own life as well as in the lives of many people I've known. People who are trapped into saying, "I can't, it just isn't possible," start saying, "How can I do it? How can I make this possible?"

Of course, that's what possibility thinking—and faith—are all about. This is what starts the wheels turning. This is what creates a "how" that you simply couldn't see or even fathom before, because you were caught in the downward cycle.

Don't Let Patience Become Procrastination

As you seek to turn the "how" into "now," it is important to see the fine line between having patience and procrastinating. Without a doubt, patience is one of the truly great virtues. One of my favorite Bible verses, in fact, says this:

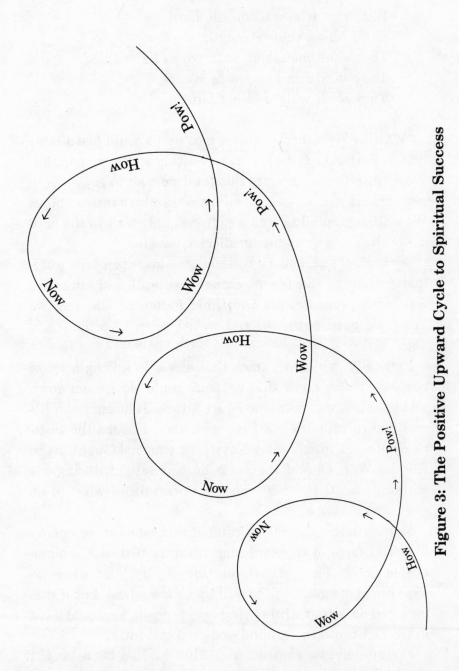

Figure 3: The Positive Upward Cycle to Spiritual Success

> But those who wait on the Lord
> Shall renew their strength;
> They shall mount up with wings like eagles,
> They shall run and not be weary,
> They shall walk and not faint.[1]

"Waiting" is something that most of us could learn to do better. Particularly in America, waiting isn't very popular. We wait in line to get into theaters; we wait to get seats in restaurants where "twenty minutes" can turn into an hour. We wait at stoplights, and we often simply wait in the middle of the freeways when gridlock closes in.

With all of our modern technology—laser printers, automatic dialing, and fax machines—we still find ourselves waiting a great deal of the time! Patience? Oh, yes, we know we need patience, and we'd like to have it—*right now!*

Ironically, while we know that stress is killing a lot of people, we also know that patience could slow them down and possibly prevent some heart attacks. Patience can literally save your life, as I learned when I heard the testimony of one United States Navy pilot who had fought in the Korean War. One of the rules he was taught during his training was that when you are uncertain of what to do next, *do nothing at all.*

Months later, he was in combat and was hit by enemy fire. The force of the explosion literally turned his plane upside down. The natural reaction of any pilot when he feels his plane get hit is to pull up on the wheel, but if this man had done that while flying upside down, he would have nosed right into the ground and died instantly.

Fortunately, he remembered what he had been taught and he did nothing at all. For several seconds he flew upside down, just getting his bearings. When he realized his situation, he calmly maneuvered his plane right side up and was then able to land safely.

There is no question that patience can be of enormous value when used wisely and accurately, but there is one problem with patience. If you aren't careful, your patience can become procrastination. Admittedly, this is a gray area; the line between patience and procrastination is a fine one. Only you can realize when you've crossed that line and your patience has become procrastination.

The Day Johnny Crean Set Me Straight

Nine years ago when I started Rancho Capistrano Community Church, we did not have the beautiful location we now enjoy. We had to search long and hard, in fact, to find any public place where we could gather, and I remember making the announcement that our first service would be held on September 27 at the Mission Drive-in Theatre at San Juan Capistrano.

Just a week before our first service, I got a notice from the city council telling us we could not hold services at the Mission Drive-in Theatre because there would be danger of traffic problems with all the extra cars. I was flattered by the city council's concern over traffic jams due to my preaching, but I was also dismayed. What could I do now? We had run down any number of other leads, and they had all been dead ends.

That notice from the city council was a great deal like the enemy fire that turned the navy pilot's plane upside down. And, like the navy pilot, I remembered to respond at first by "doing nothing at all." My problem was, however, that my doing nothing at all went on for several weeks. We had to cancel the opening date and tell people that the new date would be set "as soon as possible."

23

As the days went by, many suggestions for other places to meet were presented, but I would always find something wrong with them. One wasn't large enough, another was too far out of the way, still another seemed to conflict or compete with a church nearby. I kept finding something wrong with every location that seemed to be available, and we went on for weeks without holding our first worship service.

One morning I had breakfast with Johnny Crean, a young layman who was one of my chief supporters in trying to get the new ministry started. Johnny had something to tell me and he came right to the point: "Robert, if you wanted to, you could hold services this coming Sunday. You could do it in your living room. You could do it in your backyard. You could do it anywhere you wanted to. Robert, you're dragging your feet!"

As I looked into Johnny's flashing eyes, I knew he was right. After leaving the restaurant, I went back to my office to look again at all the alternative locations that people had suggested. One kept staring me right in the face, and I couldn't ignore it—the Saddleback Junior College gymnasium just north of San Juan Capistrano in Mission Viejo, not far from the San Diego Freeway. I drove over, looked at the gym again, and realized that it could do in a pinch—and we were definitely in a pinch.

Johnny Crean's blunt remark, made in love and concern, helped me realize I was dragging my feet. I was stalling, because I had a personal problem—fear. Many people procrastinate because they are afraid of something, and I had been afraid to face the prospect of preaching every week on an indefinite basis. Until that time, I had preached only occasionally at the Crystal Cathedral where I was on staff. There I had six weeks or more to prepare a message. Now I would have to come up with a new message every seven days, and that thought frightened me!

Nonetheless, I knew it was time to break the fear barrier and get out of my rut of procrastination before it became a grave for the new church. I realized anew what I had often told others—the best way to overcome fear is with faith.

One day, in the quiet of my study, I gave myself my own pep talk: "Faith is the assurance of things hoped for, the conviction of things not seen. If you believe you can, you can. A fighter full of faith always conquers his fears. When God says, 'Go,' put on your track shoes. Small deeds done are better than great deeds planned. It's time, Schuller, to put on your track shoes and trust God!"

We held our first service in the Saddleback College gym the very next Sunday. My fear barrier was broken, and we were off and running as a brand-new church in a strategic part of Orange County, one of the fastest growing areas in Southern California.

What I Learned About Goal Setting

Procrastinating over where and when to start a new church taught me several things about goal setting. I have often said that there is no question that God wants us to have goals. Jesus Himself said, "Ask, and it will be given to you; seek, and you will find; knock, and it will be opened to you."[2]

Many people wonder, however, "What goals should I set?" God gives us help. He directs us in several ways: "two-way prayer," Scripture, and through His Spirit bearing witness with our spirit.

By "two-way prayer," I mean prayer as a two-way communication between you and God. I practice this all the time, trying to get away where I can be in a relaxed state of mind, clear of distractions. One of my favorite places to relax is anywhere on or near the water. Water and I seem

Overcome fear
with faith.

———— • ————

to have a bond of some kind and, because I live near the ocean, I often go there to put aside the many pressures that I am facing and talk to God about what He wants me to do. I want to do His will, yes, but there always seem to be several options, and I list those options, asking Him to tell me which one is best.

I sit there and wait for a response, but it seldom comes in audible, crashing tones—a thunderous voice from the sky telling me to pick "option *B*." Instead, I get some form of assurance that I should move ahead with one of the choices. And when I get that assurance, I continue praying and ask God, "If this is what You want me to do, what's the best way to do it?" Again, there are usually several alternatives and, again, I don't hear an audible voice telling me, "Choose alternative *C*." Nonetheless, when I sit and wait, I get a conviction that tells me which one is right for me.

But I don't stop there. After all, my "conviction" might be my own bias or subjectivity. Instead, I take the next step in my decision-making process and lay the grid of Scripture over whatever goal I am thinking about pursuing. I ask, "Is this right, or does it conflict with anything that God has told us plainly?" When I search the Scriptures and find no apparent problem, I'm well on my way to knowing that I have made a good decision and that God is directing me.

But I have one more test—I go back to what originated my idea in the first place and recheck my own desires, hopes, and needs. The Psalmist tells us, "Trust in the Lord, and do good; . . . delight yourself also in the Lord, and He shall give you the desires of your heart. Commit your way to the Lord, trust also in Him, and He shall bring it to pass."[3]

As long as I am delighting myself in what God wants and trusting in Him, I can be sure that what I want isn't prompted by selfish motivations. I can also be sure that God will very likely want to give me the desires of my heart

(providing, of course, that there is not something He knows and I don't that might lead to unforeseen problems.)

After Jesus told His followers to ask, seek, and knock, He went on to ask them if there was any father among them who would give his son a stone when he asked for bread or a serpent when he asked for a piece of fish. Then Jesus added, "If you then, being evil, know how to give good gifts to your children, how much more will your Father who is in heaven give good things to those who ask Him!"[4]

Jesus was making a very simple analogy, comparing God with fathers (and mothers, too, for that matter). In effect, he was saying, "God doesn't dangle good things before our eyes and say, 'Sorry, you can't have them.' No good parent does that to his child, and God does not do that to His children, either."

But I Forgot the Most Important Part

As I set a goal to start a new church somewhere in the San Juan Capistrano area, I used all the tests I described above. But when opposition came my way, I floundered and then slipped into a comfortable "procrastination zone," telling myself that I was simply "waiting for God's further leading." The truth was that I was afraid to take on the challenge of having to prepare a sermon every week, having to run a church and deal with the multitude of problems that occur. I had forgotten the most important part about setting goals. In my pride (which led to my fear), I had forgotten the need for humility. I had forgotten to say, "Yes, Lord, I have this goal, but I really need You. I'll never reach it without You."

I was letting fear hold me in its grip, while I glossed it over by telling myself I was just "waiting on the Lord." There is a verse in the New Testament that describes the problem I had at that moment. James, the half brother of Jesus, wrote a letter to a group of people who were living in fear, frustrated because they couldn't reach their goals. He told them that they didn't have because they didn't ask. Or, when they did ask, they didn't receive because they were asking amiss. James told them to submit to God and draw near to Him so He would draw near to them. Then he added, "Humble yourselves in the sight of the Lord, and He will lift you up."[5]

The very beginning of reaching any goal is humility. You begin by knowing that you are small in God's sight and that you reach your goals only through His help. God wants you to succeed, but only on His terms, not yours.

The best thing about succeeding on God's terms is that he doesn't hem us in. When we pursue goals that He wants for our lives, He opens doors of opportunity that we never even imagined. That is exactly what happened to me when I decided to go ahead with that first service. We met in the Saddleback College gymnasium for eighteen months, and then, through a series of circumstances that only God could have engineered, we were allowed to use part of the Rancho Capistrano property to construct a permanent church home.

Your Success May Be Large—or Small

As you set goals and start to reach them, "now" becomes a "wow." You start to see results and hear yourself saying, "Wow! Look what's happening. The desires that God has given me are beginning to unfold. It's all becoming a reality. Look at the people who are getting on my team. Look at the steps of success that I've been able to take."

With the momentum moving in this cycle, "wow" becomes "pow." Maybe the rhyme is a little corny, but nonetheless it describes what real success is all about. "Pow"—you've done it! You *did* succeed, even if it was just a small taste. The great thing about this positive upward success cycle is that it doesn't have to apply only to people who move from a life of poverty to becoming billionaires. The success cycle can include basic, everyday challenges, such as training yourself to get to work on time or pulling off a special dinner party for several friends on a Saturday night.

Finally, the cycle comes full swing when the "pow" of success gives us the resources to stretch our faith and ask "how?" when previously we would not dare to even venture into that realm. The "pow" becomes a "how." (I will go into greater detail of how the cycle creates an ongoing upward movement in chapter 8. Make sure you read it!)

Have You Ever Tried to Clap With One Hand?

The success cycle can even work regarding something as simple as applauding an entertainer. The late Jimmy Durante was one of the greatest comedians who ever lived. During World War II, Ed Sullivan asked Jimmy if he would come to a veterans' hospital and entertain some of the soldiers who had been wounded.

"Ed," Jimmy said, "I'd love to accept, but I've got two engagements at a radio station at that very same time, I just can't pass them up. They offer tremendous remuneration for me, and I can't afford to pass them by."

Being a possibility thinker in his own right, Ed Sullivan started asking the question, "How? How can we get Jimmy to entertain the wounded veterans and still make it possible for him to make those other engagements?"

As Sullivan considered his possibilities, he figured out a way for Jimmy Durante to come and be the first one on the program at the veterans' hospital.

"We'll get you in and then scoot you off right away, and

you'll still be able to make your radio appearances. You can do both!"

"Great!" said Jimmy, and he agreed to come and entertain the wounded men.

Jimmy Durante went on first as planned, and he was never better. He had the men roaring with laughter, and you could almost feel their spirits rising higher and higher. When he finished his routine, he got tremendous applause—a standing ovation (by those who could stand).

Then the men cheered for more. Jimmy paused for a few brief seconds. He seemed to be watching two men in the front row who were joining enthusiastically in the applause.

Hesitating no longer, he graciously agreed to stay and give a second performance. Again, he kept the entire room in stitches and when he finished the second routine, the men applauded even louder and cheered him on, shouting, "Encore, encore!" Unbelievably, Jimmy Durante stayed for a third performance before he finally gave up the stage.

When Jimmy came off, Ed Sullivan took him aside and said, "Jimmy, that was absolutely wonderful. You'll never know how much good you did these men. But now you've missed your radio engagements. Why did you decide to stay to give the second and third performances?"

Jimmy Durante looked at Ed Sullivan, and then he pointed out at the crowd, "Just look in the front row." And there Ed Sullivan saw two soldiers who were still applauding Jimmy's fantastic work. Both of them had lost an arm at the elbow, but they were still applauding by clapping together, using the one good hand each man had left.

I believe those men are a symbol of the upward cycle of success. They didn't just say, "We can't—we can't applaud, we can't do anything. We're amputees." Instead they said, "How can we do something to show our appreciation?"

First, they turned "how" into "now" and seized the moment to join in thanking a great entertainer for a lift that was so badly needed by themselves as well as all their comrades.

Next, in a simple act of joining what resources they had, these two men turned "how" into "wow," and, finally, "wow" turned into "pow." They succeeded in doing what some would have thought was impossible.

The two amputees touched Jimmy Durante's heart so much that he decided on the spot to give up the engagements that could have made him a lot of money. Instead, he put financial gain aside for something greater. *That* is what true success is all about.

Turning "I can't" into "How can I?" is not some psychological gimmick that originated in the twentieth century. It has been with us at least as long as men have walked the earth. It's a principle you can find throughout the Bible where people turned dreams into realities. They turned visions God had given them into success. They didn't say, "Well, I've failed again, I can't do anything, I'm stuck, and I might as well give up." Instead they asked, "What can I do today? What tiny step can I take to make the dreams God has given me come true?"

William James said, "The greatest factor in any undertaking is belief in it." I like that, but I like what the Apostle Paul said even more: "I can do all things through Christ who strengthens me."[6] The greatest factor in any undertaking is our belief in God. He gives us what we need so that we can believe in ourselves and in what He has given us to accomplish.

Possibility thinking (faith) always says, "How can I turn the 'how' into a 'now'? What can I do today to get the wheels moving?" The amazing thing about being on a positive upward cycle is that once you start to make your moves, then all kinds of things can happen. Sometimes you have to make quick decisions, but because you're on the right kind of roll, you are given the wisdom and the power to do so.

Now Gay Is on the Upward Cycle

Today when I talk with Gay, she is a new and different woman. From that tiny beginning on that desperate day when she first came to see us many months ago, Gay decided to set some goals to help turn "how" into "now." Ever since childhood, she had felt that church was where she should be. When no one took her to church, she would take herself or go with one of her young friends. Their church became her church because she knew that there was something good and decent about it, and that people involved in church had something special going for them that she didn't have.

Later, because of some wrong choices, she had drifted away and had fallen into her failure cycle. But when she came to see us, she was determined to increase her spiritual understanding and desire. She set several goals to ensure that she would not continue on the downward cycle of failure.

First, she made a full commitment to her spiritual life by joining Rancho Capistrano and faithfully attending worship services every week. She also determined to serve God in whatever ways He would open up to her. Today Gay is the organizational secretary of the Women's Guild of our church.

Another goal for Gay was to build a successful marriage. During the ensuing months, she married a fine man who gave her the security and love she had never had.

People who knew Gay in the past now tell her, "Isn't this wonderful? Years ago things weren't right, and now look at what's happened. You have a nice husband and a new home but, even more important, you're happier. You've got a good attitude and enjoy your work. I'm so glad things are different for you."

Now Gay's family life feels permanent for the first time. She told me, "All the counseling I had ever received before

33

had not worked. I would give them my money, cry for an hour, tell them what was wrong, and leave. But what I learned from my counseling at Rancho Capistrano was to turn it over to God. I learned to give it *all* to Him—all the stress, all the garbage, why I couldn't sleep, why I cried so much. I learned to picture it in my mind—actually see myself handing it all over to God."

Gay is quick to point out that she's a long way from some kind of "pinnacle of perfection," but she is on a roll; she is progressing. She still struggles daily, but now when pressures come, she knows what to do.

"Sometimes I feel myself wanting to give up, or I can tell I'm slipping back into rationalizing and justifying failure," she says. "Sometimes I feel myself getting angry and wanting to bark at people. But no matter what it is, I just give it back to God. I give Him all the mistakes that I couldn't handle that day. Before, when I tried to control my life myself, it never worked. I'd play 'Crisis Christian'—going to God with a major problem and then dumping Him as soon as I thought I could manage. Now, I just hand it *all* to Him on a daily basis."

Gay tells me she represents millions of people out there, and I know she's right. No matter how bad things can get, there is no need to stay trapped in a downward cycle of spiritual failure. Refuse to keep on telling yourself, "I can't. I'm stuck. I'm lost!"

Instead, rely on age-old principles that tell you that with God all things are possible.[7] Realize that through God you can do all things because you have His strength.[8]

As your faith continues to work, what you have hoped for—what has not been visible—will appear.[9] And God will do more than you ever asked or imagined because His power is at work in you!

Chapter 2
As You Think, You
Will Be

Are you an optimist or a pessimist? There is a well-worn story about parents who had two sons, one an incurable optimist and the other a complete pessimist. Christmas came and they decided to give the pessimist a beautiful new mountain bike to cheer him up. Unfortunately, he soon found a tiny scratch on the frame and proceeded to complain about the bike's not being any good.

Noting that their pessimist son was operating true to form, the parents checked on their optimist, to whom they had given a giant box of pony manure. They found him playing happily in the mess, with a big smile on his face.

Marveling at his optimism, his father asked, "Son, how can you be so happy when all we gave you was a box of manure?"

"Easy, Dad," the boy said. "With all this manure, there's got to be a pony in here somewhere!"

I've told this story many times, and it seldom fails to get

a good response, even from people I know I've told it to before. There is something within most of us that admires optimism. Optimism is the door to achievement and feeling good about life, while pessimism is a dead end.

Uncle Jay—the Classic Pessimist

Surprising as it may seem, I have a negative relative whom I'll call Uncle Jay. To label Uncle Jay, who is now in his seventies, a pessimist might be understating it a bit. We had a family gathering not too long ago and I had an enlightening conversation with him. As we sat down together, I said, "Uncle Jay, how are you doing?"

"Oh, I don't know."

"What does that mean?"

"Well, it's just the way it is. I don't know."

Having gotten off to this rousing and articulate start, I plunged ahead. Because Uncle Jay was retired and living in another part of the state, I thought it might be interesting to find out what his normal routine was like. "Uncle Jay, what is your normal day like? What do you do during the day?"

"Well, I get up in the morning. . . ." Uncle Jay paused, acting as though he had answered my question.

"Yes," I urged, "and do you have breakfast?"

"No, I don't like breakfast."

"What do you do then?"

"Well, I used to get up and sit and watch television, but I don't like TV anymore. There aren't any good programs."

"I see. Well, perhaps you go out for walks?"

"Oh, no, no. What would the neighbors think? If they saw me out walking around, they might think I lost something or who knows what?"

"So, what do you do all day?"

"Well, I sit."

"You sit?"

"Yes . . . I sit."

"Well, Uncle Jay, why do you just sit all day?"

"Because I don't want to stand all day."

(I give you my word, this is an honest-to-goodness conversation I had with my Uncle Jay.) Undaunted, I asked, "Well, Uncle Jay, have you thought of exercising? I understand it's important for human beings to exercise because it keeps the heart fit. What do you do for exercise?"

"Oh, I don't do anything."

"Don't you realize you might get a heart attack if you don't exercise that heart muscle regularly?" I asked in wonderment.

"Oh, that would be terrific. Then all my problems would be over."

"Your problems? What problems do you have?"

"Oh, I don't know. . . ."

I'm not sure what prompted my next remark. Perhaps I was a bit exasperated with the hopeless tenor of our conversation. Anyway, I said, "You know, Uncle Jay, with modern medicine the way it is, chances are, if you had a heart attack they would probably revive you before you went. Not only that, but you could wind up a semi-invalid and find yourself in a nursing home."

Suddenly Uncle Jay's absolutely placid look turned to one of consternation: "Oh, I wouldn't like that at all."

"I believe that. Uncle Jay, why don't you call one of your neighbors and see if he'll go for a walk with you? Why not try to start walking regularly?"

Uncle Jay looked at me for a few seconds, and then from his lips came the only faintly positive remark he made all day:

"Maybe I will."

Uncle Jay Is Trapped in a Downward Cycle

"Maybe I will." I had to be content with that from Uncle Jay. That was as optimistic as he could become in one conversation. I checked back later and learned, not to my surprise, that Uncle Jay never did start walking. He continues to sit all day, because he doesn't want to stand. He's trapped in the negative downward cycle that begins with pessimism, drifts into lethargy, and winds up in defeat. The defeat creates more pessimism and the cycle starts a downward spiral (*see* Figure 4). Uncle Jay just might be the most startling example of this downward cycle I've ever met.

The pessimist is convinced that things are never going to go his way, that life has dealt him a bad hand. He never takes a chance, never attempts anything risky—or even mildly challenging. Uncle Jay fits all these descriptions to a *P*—for PESSIMISM.

In an article entitled, "Do Optimists Live Longer?"[1] Nan Silver reports on studies made by University of Pennsylvania psychologist, Martin Seligman, who joined with two other scientists to study the thinking and speech of ninety-nine veterans of World War II. From their findings, they have advanced a provocative theory claiming that optimists live longer and are healthier while pessimists have chronically poor health and die younger.

According to the research, optimists and pessimists differ tremendously in their explanatory style—that is, how they explain the events in their lives, including anything from winning at Scrabble to running a red light and getting a ticket. When pessimists talk, they reveal three telltale characteristics:

1. They assume their problems are never-ending or what researchers call "stable." They believe they *always* had a certain problem and they *always* will.

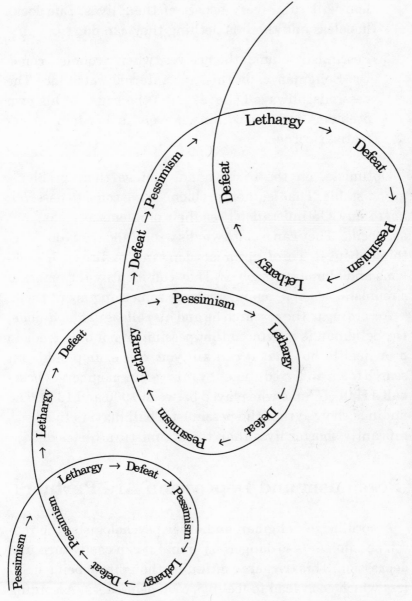

Figure 4: The Negative Downward Cycle to Thinking Failure

2. Pessimists believe that the cause of their problem is global, rather than specific. In other words, their problem will ruin every aspect of their lives. Life looks hopeless and there is nothing they can do.

3. Pessimists blame themselves when troubles come. Dr. Seligman calls this an "internal" attitude. The pessimist always believes he is the cause of his own problems and thinks himself even further into the defeatist's corner.

Optimists, on the other hand, believe their problems aren't stable. That is, their problems have come to pass, *but not to stay*. Optimists don't see their problems as global, but as specific. They can isolate what's wrong and try to do something about it. Third, optimists don't internalize their problems and blame themselves. They can identify the external circumstances and, again, try to do something about them.

According to the research he and his colleagues have done, Dr. Seligman is convinced that pessimism not only leads to poor health, but that it can kill you. For example, his research team analyzed quotes by thirty-four members of baseball's Hall of Fame who played between 1900 and 1950. The findings showed that the pessimistic ball players lived significantly shorter lives than the optimistic athletes did.[2]

Pessimism and Depression Are Partners

According to Seligman and other psychologists, the reason pessimism is so dangerous is that it can easily turn into depression. This triggers continuing thoughts of being helpless which soon lead to feelings of hopelessness. According to Seligman, ". . . people who develop an 'I surrender' attitude are less likely to take care of themselves, eat right, see doctors, or seek support from family and friends."[3]

Problems have come to pass, not to stay.

———— ◆ ————

Obviously, when I read this article, I immediately thought of my conversation with Uncle Jay. He has definitely developed an "I surrender" attitude. He believes his problems will never end (except with death). And his lethargy has ruined all aspects of his life. Now he just sits, making as little effort as possible. Setting any kind of goal, making any kind of plan, or taking even the simplest action all seem repugnant, or at least totally uninteresting.

Actually, Uncle Jay is well beyond lethargy. He has become fatalistic and "resigned to his fate." I have talked to many people in a negative downward cycle of thinking, and they often mention that they wish they could have been *luckier* in life. As a rule, people who wish they'd been luckier are seldom people who have any concept of God or of trusting Him. This secular humanist approach to life substitutes the word *luck* for what God is doing. Since the secular humanist doesn't believe in God or even think about Him much, he has to use some other term—like *luck*.

According to the dictionary, *luck* is the fortuitous happening of fortunate or adverse events, your fortune or your lot. There is no mention of the Deity. When the secular humanist uses the word *luck,* I think to myself, *You're telling me how God works in a world where you think there is no God.*

If luck controls your life, you can easily slip into a negative downward cycle, particularly if your "luck goes bad." On the other hand, if you want to think your way to success at any level, you have to begin with God, knowing that He's at work within you. Then luck becomes something else. It becomes looking to Christ for guidance, understanding God's love, and calling out to Christ for help, knowing that God will see you through.

When you have all that going for you, you don't have to worry about having good or bad "luck." You rest secure in knowing that God will provide what you need.

Think Success—Be a Success

The power of the mind is awesome. I've always been fascinated by psychologists' assertions that we use less than 10 percent of our mental powers. Think what we could do if we put the other 90 percent into action!

As powerful as the mind is, however, it is at the mercy of a four-inch network of cells radiating from your brain stem, which is called the *reticular activating system*. Dr. Denis Waitley, the behavioral psychologist who is in continual demand by some of the biggest corporations in the world for his motivational and productivity speeches and seminars, calls the reticular activating system the RAS, for short.

Waitley compares the RAS to a little robot who is posted in your mind as a

> ... sentinel who is responsible for filtering all incoming stimuli, everything from sights and sounds to smells and touches. Nothing gets past RAS unless permission is granted. RAS determines moment by moment which information is going to become part of you. In other words, RAS is the one who is really in control of your to-do list and your priorities. RAS decides what habits you break or form.[4]

Waitley believes that the RAS is not a tyrant but actually our slave, doing exactly what we want him to do—emphasizing what is really important to us. As Waitley puts it,

> ... your reticular activating system never tells you what to do. You are in charge, and it does only what you ask. It will take negative or positive input, and the only thing it is concerned about is *how important that input is to you* [italics mine, added for emphasis]."[5]

Understanding a little bit about how the RAS works dramatically demonstrates how important it is to be optimistic rather than pessimistic about life. If you go around telling yourself that you're just unlucky, or it's just "my fate," you will probably wind up on a negative downward cycle of failure. Do you know anyone who is accident-prone? More often than not, accident-prone people are the pessimistic types who keep telling themselves, "I'm just a klutz—I can't help it."

When a mother admonishes her small child to "Never put beans in your ears!" she usually only succeeds in programming him to do just that. Why? Because the child's RAS tells him, "Mom thinks this is really important. I should try it."

Whenever I try to lose weight, I'm doomed to failure if I tell myself, "I'm *not* going to eat today." All that does is make me think about food practically every minute. When I tell myself I'm not going to eat today, my RAS knows that food is very important to me, and that is precisely why I think about it all day long. On the other hand, if I pack my calendar with activities, and possibly even work through lunch, my RAS has other things to deal with. I don't think about food and it's easier to control my intake of calories.

As Denis Waitley says,

> Your RAS can be programmed to tune in on success and failure. The RAS helps explain why some people are failure-prone and others are success-prone. It explains why some people see a problem in every suggested solution and others see a solution for every problem.

Does God Prefer Pessimism or Optimism?

I believe that God much prefers that we be optimists rather than pessimists. That's why the Bible is so full of teachings and principles about having hope and seeking the more abundant life. How, then, do we become the optimistic people God intends us to be? We can begin by remembering what King Solomon wrote about being a happy person: "Happy the man [or woman] who puts his trust in the Lord."[6] Here in the words of the king who was called the wisest man on earth is the biblical foundation for being optimistic. It is a principle you can use in any situation, whether circumstances are good or bad.

Another verse of Scripture—possibly the best-known passage in the entire Bible—also applies here. Several years ago my father was executive director of the *Possibility Thinker's Bible*. He marked hundreds of "positive verses for possibility thinking" by having them highlighted in blue ink. Not surprisingly, John 3:16 was among them: "For God so loved the world that He gave His only begotten Son, that whoever believes in Him should not perish but have everlasting life."

As wonderful as this promise is, it becomes even more powerful when you read the verse that follows: "For God did not send His Son into the world to condemn the world, but that the world through Him might be saved."

Together these two verses give any believer in Jesus Christ the ultimate reason to be optimistic. He who believes in Christ is not judged. The foundational meaning of the Christian faith is that Christ went to the Cross to take all of God's judgment for sin on Himself. God does not judge His children because they have already been judged through Jesus Christ.

One of the saddest news accounts I ever read told of a Filipino man named Gerardo Calubag, who murdered three people, stabbed dozens of others, and ended up on death row in prison. While asleep in his cell in the maximum security New Bilibid Prison in suburban Manila, Gerardo had a vision that told him to follow in Christ's footsteps and suffer crucifixion. On every Good Friday thereafter, Gerardo would carry a twenty-foot-long, fifty-pound cross throughout the prison compound for more than an hour; then he would lay on the cross as fellow inmates pounded four-inch nails through his hands and feet and hoisted him into the air, where he would remain on the cross for at least fifteen minutes in the broiling sun.

Gerardo claims that while on the cross, he feels no pain. In his mind, being crucified every Good Friday helps him deal with the guilt that he still feels about the crimes he has committed. He believes God has taught him how to repent for what he did and says, "In a way, it feels good. I feel contentment and peace with myself."[7]

Poor Gerardo. Every Good Friday he suffers needless pain because he doesn't realize that he is negating Christ's sacrifice on the Cross, which was done *once*— for *all* sin. He is placing his faith in his own sacrifice rather than in what Christ has done.

If God does not continue to judge us for our sins, why should we? Why should we go on with a pessimistic attitude, believing the world is falling apart, when God has given us every reason to believe the world is holding together? What greater reason for optimism could there be than that?

Problems Come to Pass, Not to Stay

The Bible contains many verses that explain why the negative downward cycle of pessimism, lethargy, and defeat can be changed to a positive upward cycle: optimism, decisiveness, and persistence (*see* Figure 5).

Your first step to this upward cycle is to remember that problems pass. No matter how difficult or sticky things get, the circumstances and all of the accompanying frustrations

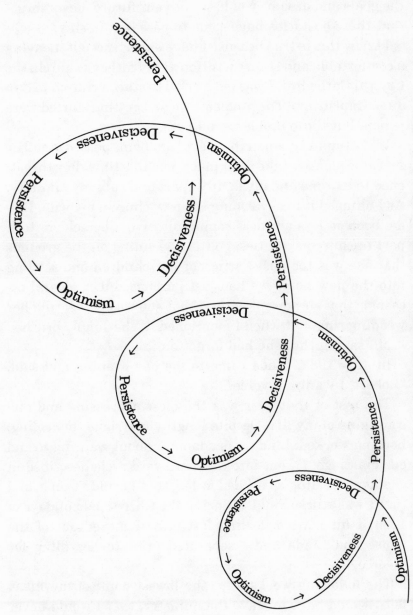

Figure 5: The Positive Upward Cycle to Thinking Success

will pass. No matter what obstacles stand between you and the goals and dreams you have for your future, never forget that these obstacles have come to pass, not to stay.

I know this is true because I have experienced it. Leaving a comfortable and secure position at my father's church, the Crystal Cathedral, I was led by God to start a church in San Juan Capistrano. The problems we had getting started were legion, but those problems did pass.

Unfortunately, when that set of problems passed, another set came along to take their place, and this time they threatened to tear me and my family apart and ruin my ministry. As I plunged into developing the new church, my wife, Linda, became less and less communicative. She seldom took part in church activities, politely declining on the grounds that she was too busy caring for our children and settling into the new home we had just purchased. On several occasions that summer, I noticed that she wasn't wearing her wedding ring, but when I mentioned it, she simply brushed it off, saying that she had forgotten it.

In July 1983, Linda came to me one evening and said, "Robert, I want a divorce."

The rest of that year was the most depressing and discouraging of my life. Despite lengthy marriage counseling, nothing worked. Linda was adamant about wanting to end our marriage. I went into the downward cycle described in chapter 1, feeling as if I had failed, that I couldn't cope, and that I was stuck. Finally, during the Christmas holidays of 1983, I hit bottom, feeling lost after I moved out of the house and Linda and I separated prior to her filing for divorce.

The following weeks were the lowest point of my life. I felt I would have to leave the ministry, that I would never marry again, and that I would spend the rest of my life alone, visiting my children only occasionally. My life was ruined, my career was over. I was unqualified to be a spiritual leader of others. Ministers don't go through divorces if they're any good—or so I told myself.

During those months of struggle, there were times when I was often tempted to despair and give in to total pessimism. But possibility thinking kept me on the side of optimism. I hung on, clinging to a life preserver that was labeled "Happy the man who trusts in the Lord."

And somehow the problems did pass! Instead of rejecting me, my church congregation gathered around me in unbelieving love and concern. My father encouraged me, telling me the story of another minister whose marriage had fallen apart and how he had faced a choice: fulfill the call God had given him, or quit and walk away. I'll never forget my father's words, spoken very slowly as if he were choosing each one: "You can continue on. Your congregation will support you. Just allow God to work in your life."

God did work, in ways too wonderful to be true. The entire story is recorded in two of my books, *Getting Through the Going-Through Stage* and *Power to Grow Beyond Yourself.*[8] Today I am happily remarried to Donna and the father of two more wonderful children—Christina, who is now four and a half, and Anthony, now three.

Focus on the Problem—Then Solve It

After assuring yourself that problems do pass, use your optimism as a springboard to decisiveness—focusing on exactly what your problem is so you can solve it.

All too often I meet people—many of whom have come for counseling—who are muddling around, caught in their web of problems and pain, but with no idea of what step to take next.

When I just couldn't find a place to start holding services for the new church, I was caught in this trap. When Johnny

Crean forced me to face my procrastination, I realized I had to focus on my real problem—being afraid to take on the weekly responsibility of preaching and pastoring that would start once that first service was held.

When Gay came to see us for counseling, she was overwhelmed with an incredible array of problems and unfortunate circumstances that had gone on for years. She knew something had to change, and as we counseled her, she saw that her real problem was not any particular hassle or calamity that she had been facing. Her real problem was the dysfunctional syndrome that she had coped with all her life because of a history of alcoholism in her family that went back three generations. But once Gay decided that the whole world wasn't against her and that she *could* survive, she was able to start dealing with and solving her problems, one at a time.

The most dramatic illustration of focusing on your problem and solving it that I've ever seen, however, was my sister, Carol, who was in a motorcycle accident that almost cost her her life. While visiting our uncle's farm in Iowa, Carol went for a motorcycle ride with our cousin and, as they zoomed over the crest of a hill, they came up behind a car that had stopped directly in their path. With split seconds to make a decision, my cousin swerved into the other lane to avoid the vehicle in his path. He didn't see an oncoming car and they collided head-on.

Carol was knocked from the motorcycle and flew some seventy feet through the air, landing in a ditch that happened to be right in front of a slaughterhouse. Her foot was crushed and doctors immediately had to amputate up to the shin. She also suffered a compound fracture of her thigh, and the splintered fragments of bone were covered with mud that was filled with bacteria, which had grown there in the spilled blood from thousands of slaughtered animals.

The bacteria caused raging infections in her body which

baffled the doctors as they used numerous antibiotics, most of which had zero effect. They admitted Carol was suffering infections that they had never seen before. At times her life literally hung in the balance.

I'll never forget going to the hospital with my father and watching him take Carol's hand and say quietly to her, "Carol, your blood consists of red blood cells and white blood cells. The white blood cells are the ones that can cure you. Every single one of those white blood cells is a little soldier, and they are going to conquer and defeat the infection in your body. Carol, close your eyes right now and picture all those little soldiers marching together toward that infection to defeat it."

As Carol lay there, immobilized in traction, she closed her eyes and imagined the little white soldiers marching forward to battle the infection. This ritual went on every day for many weeks—my father assuring Carol that she could win while she focused on how the white blood cells were defeating the infection.

Carol couldn't get well in one day. She spent, in fact, 270 days in the hospital, but eventually she did triumph. She could have let the horrible injury and baffling infection wipe her out, but instead she focused on fighting her problem and defeating it. When Carol left the hospital, the doctors admitted that it was not the antibiotics that cured her infections. It was the positive focus she had on getting well.

Divide Your Problems—and Conquer

The third step on the upward cycle is to deal with problems one at a time, never take them on all at once. Jacob Riis, an American journalist, handled his problems that way. Whenever things got overwhelming, he would go out and watch stonecutters at work. He would watch the stonecutter take his chisel and his hammer and start to work away at a seemingly indestructible stone. The stonecutter would hit the chisel with his hammer and nothing would happen. Not even one tiny mark would appear on the stone. But, then, on that hundred and first blow of the hammer upon the chisel, the stone would crack open.

It's the same with problems. You can whack away at them a bit at a time and seem to be getting nowhere. But on that hundred and first time the problem cracks open and you see the solution. The optimistic person deals with his or her problems one at a time, little by little, and eventually those problems are solved.

But let me offer an important word of caution. It takes patient persistence to keep hammering away at your problems. One of the best statements I've ever seen on persistence was a favorite saying of Ray Kroc, the creator and developer of the world-famous McDonald's hamburger franchise chain:

> Press on: nothing in the world can take the place of persistence. Talent will not; nothing is more common than unsuccessful individuals with talent. Genius will not; unrewarded genius is almost a proverb. Education will not: the world is full of educated derelicts. Persistence and determination alone are omnipotent.[9]

That is a fabulous statement, but I like to amend it with one additional thought from the Scriptures. Persistence, determination, *and faith* make an omnipotent combination. To paraphrase the words of the Apostle Paul, "You can work out your problems with persistence and determination, but only because you know that God is at work within you, willing and doing what He wants because He knows what is best for you."[10]

Chapter 3
Manage Your Moods or They'll Manage You

It's time for a quiz. What is the world's Number One Public Health Problem? Is it:

   a.   Cancer
   b.   Depression
   c.   Heart disease

According to medical doctor David D. Burns, the answer is *b*—depression. He writes:

> . . . depression is so wide-spread it is considered the common cold of psychiatric disturbances. But there is a grim difference between depression and a cold. Depression can kill you. The suicide rate, studies indicate, has been on a shocking increase in recent years, even among children and adolescents. This escalating death rate has occurred in spite of the billions of anti-depressant drugs and tranquilizers that have been dispensed during the past several decades.[1]

Dr. Burns is one of a group of psychiatrists and psychologists at the University of Pennsylvania School of Medicine, which has been developing a revolutionary treatment for depression called *cognitive therapy*. The theory behind cognitive therapy is simple: How you think can profoundly influence how you feel.

I recall spending a week in a seminar taught by Dr. Burns on the island of Maui in Hawaii. On that occasion he centered on teaching us how to communicate when dealing with criticism. You can let criticism tear you apart, or you can try to understand the person making the criticism and disarm that individual with a nondefensive response. It all depends on how you want to think about it. I learned valuable lessons that week, which I've never forgotten.

You Feel What You Think

We have already looked at how negative thinking can drive you into a negative cycle of failure. In this chapter, we'll see why negative thinking has such a powerful influence on your emotions.

Moods and emotions are crucial parts of our lives. For many people, they can go up and down like a roller coaster. Others have what are known as "mood swings."

According to Dr. David Burns,

The first principle of cognitive therapy is that *all* your moods are created by your "cognitions," or thoughts. A cognition refers to the way you look at things—your perceptions, mental attitudes, and beliefs. It includes the way you interpret things—what you say about something or someone to yourself. You *feel* the way you do right now because of the *thoughts you are thinking at this moment.*[2]

In other words, you can think yourself into feeling good—or feeling bad. It's up to you.

Another principle from cognitive therapy is that when you let yourself get into that negative downward cycle of feeling depressed, your thoughts are literally dominated by pervasive negativity. You begin to think that things will never change, a sure sign of the pessimistic outlook on life, as we saw in the last chapter. You actually *believe* that life is really bad and won't ever get any better. That's when your pain drives you into self-centeredness, looking for relief but just knowing that you won't be able to find any. Then, when others grow impatient with you and reject you, the problems and pain only increase, and so the cycle spirals downward (*see* Figure 6).

All this is a sign of distorted and illogical thinking. Your thoughts may seem rational and valid to you. In fact, you may say, "I'm just being realistic and facing facts." The truth is, facing facts with this attitude can be disastrous.

I know from personal experience how the negative cycle of emotional failure can drag you down. It usually starts with problems, which cause pain. And because pain can be so all-encompassing, whether it is emotional or physical, this moves you to a state of self-centered thinking. You are worried only about yourself and your pain and how you can get rid of it, or at least alleviate it. But as you continue on your self-centered track, you find that people aren't drawn to you. In fact, they reject you and so you continue your downward slide.

The downward cycle of problems, pain, self-centeredness, and rejection never clutched at me more viciously than during the last weeks of 1983 and the first few days of 1984, as I prepared to share with my congregation that my marriage was, indeed, ending.

When I got up that Sunday morning early in January to tell my congregation that my wife had filed for divorce just

Figure 6: The Negative Downward Cycle to Emotional Failure

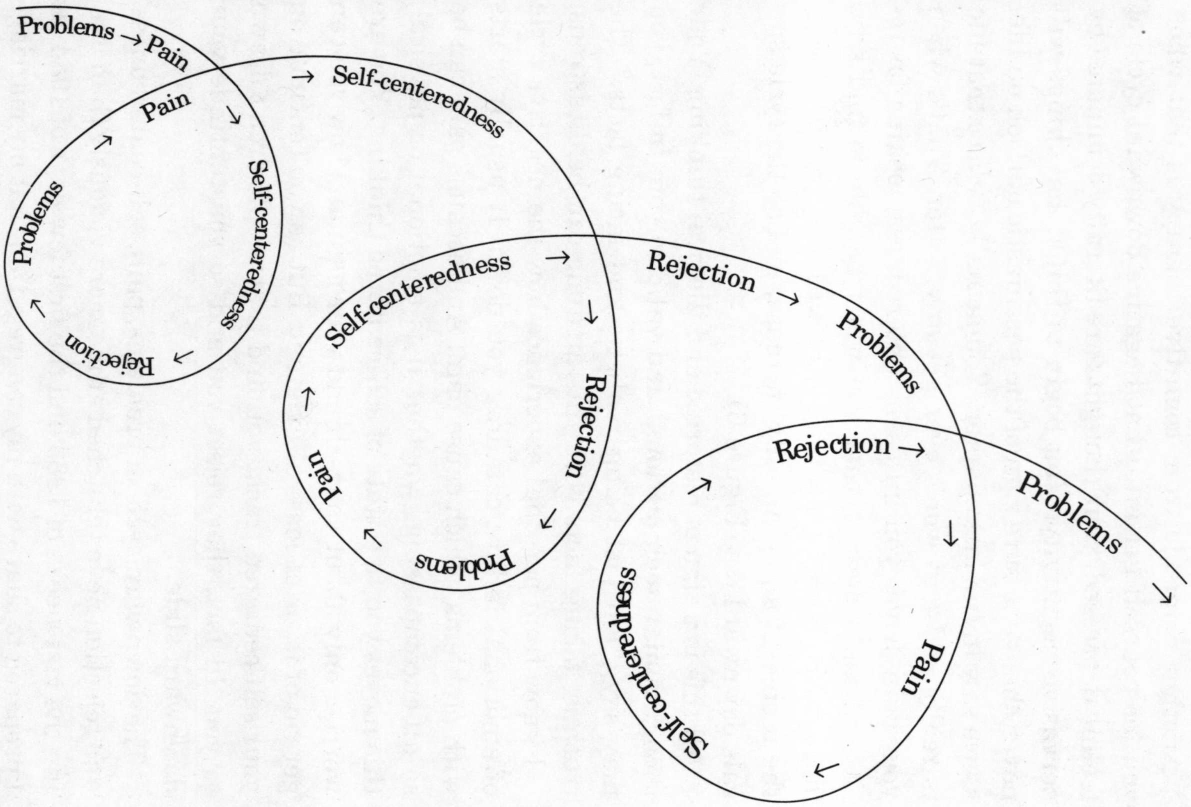

two days earlier, it was the worst hour of my life. After the service, I sat behind the pulpit, my face buried in my hands, sure that it was all over. The cycle of problems, pain, self-centeredness, and rejection had taken its full toll.

In this case my self-centeredness wasn't so much self-indulgence as it was centering on myself and my problems. The result was that I had rejected myself. No one could have been harder on me at that moment then I was.

But, amazingly, my own people didn't reject me. Dozens of them came forward to hug me, weep with me, and tell me they loved me and wanted to help—that we would all go through this together. At that moment I was still overwhelmed with grief, guilt, and pain, but a fresh ray of hope started to glimmer. Was there a way out after all? I chose to believe there was and during the following months that simple choice made all the difference.

A Loose Rudder Can Sink You

For every downward cycle that will drag you to failure, there is a positive cycle that can halt your plunge and reverse the process, starting you on an upward path. The upward cycle that rescued me consists of three simple things: trust, love, and rejoicing.

As you will note in Figure 7, the upward cycle still begins with problems. We can never escape problems, but when problems come, we can choose to respond to them in a positive way. That positive sequence begins with trust—knowing that "all things work together for good to those who love God, to those who are called according to His purpose."[3]

This is one of the most powerful biblical thoughts that you can ever run through your mind, particularly when seemingly insurmountable problems throw your life com-

Figure 7: The Positive Upward Cycle to Emotional Success

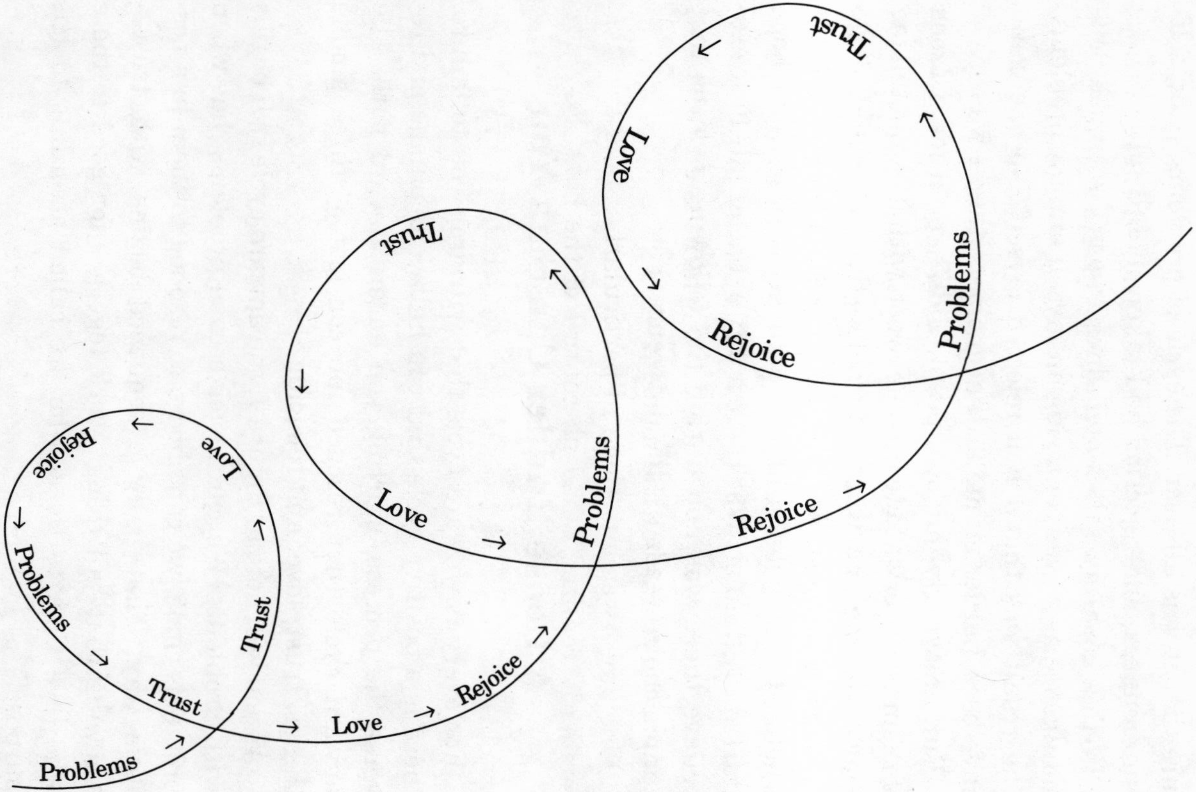

pletely out of control. At times like this, you may think you have lost your rudder, but turning to God and trusting Him can put you back on course.

As I said earlier, I love the ocean and, whenever I can, I try to get on the water because it's one place where I can forget all about the pressures that threatened to engulf me. A pastor's job is one that he usually takes home with him, and I'm no exception. I live with my job twenty-four hours a day, praying for people, talking to people, trying to help them work out solutions to their problems. Many of the problems just don't go away. The people I'm trying to help have to learn to live with them, and because these people are dear to me, I have to learn to live with them as well. During times when I just have to get away to relieve my stress, I find that if I can get out on the ocean, I can forget about everything for the moment.

One day I was out alone in particularly rough seas and suddenly realized I had no control of the boat. For some reason, the rudder would not respond. After nearly being capsized by a giant swell, I learned that the only way I could control the boat was with the twin propellers that drove it. As the boat was tossed this way and that by the waves, I learned to ease up on one throttle and accelerate the other to bring it back on course.

It took a while, but I managed to get the boat back into harbor and anchored. I went below and found that two bolts had come loose, causing the rudder to become a totally "free-wheeling" mechanism. I tightened the bolts, fastening them down with an extra hard twist, and went back to see if it had made any difference. Sure enough, the boat responded beautifully to the rudder, and I was able to leave the harbor and go back out into the swells where I had no trouble, because now my rudder kept me in control of my course.

I believe that in a very real sense, God is the rudder who controls our course. If we forget or ignore Him, it is just like having loose bolts. We will drift aimlessly and be in danger of capsizing. We may face rough seas, but if we remember that God is in control and is working out everything for our good because we love Him, we will always come through in good shape.

All That God Does Is Done Well

The most famous book of Jewish wisdom is the Talmud, which contains many wise teachings and stories. One of these stories involves a pious rabbi named Akiba. The rabbi journeyed to a far country, taking with him three incongruous possessions—an ass, a rooster, and a lamp.

When he arrived, however, he didn't get a very hospitable reception. He tried to find lodging in a village, but the citizens drove him away, and he was forced to sleep that night in a forest. But Akiba was a holy and pious man, and he responded to all this misfortune by saying simply, "All that God does is done well."

Lying down under a tree to try to get some rest, Akiba lit his lamp because he wanted to read the Torah before retiring.[4]

But the wind began whipping through the woods and blew so fiercely that it extinguished his lamp and he had to go to sleep early without getting much reading done.

Nor was that the end of his troubles. Later in the night, some wild animals passed by and chased away his rooster, undoubtedly turning him into a quick snack. Still later in the night, thieves sneaked in and stole his ass.

Things were not going well at all. But Rabbi Akiba said, "All that God does is done well."

The next morning he decided to try going back to the village to get some help. There he learned that soldiers had attacked during the night and killed everyone in the village. Had he been sleeping in the inn where he had tried to find shelter, he would have died as well.

A survivor also told him that after the bloodthirsty soldiers had finished their pillaging, they left, going in the direction of the same part of the forest where the rabbi had slept. Somehow they had missed him. Had they seen the light of his lamp in the darkness, or had they heard his rooster crow or his ass bray, they undoubtedly would have discovered him and killed him.

Rabbi Akiba thought on all these things and then he said, "All that God does is done well."

In his excellent book, simply entitled *Waiting,* Ben Patterson relates Rabbi Akiba's story and adds:

> Once in a while we are permitted the perspective on our lives and on our sufferings that was permitted Rabbi Akiba. But usually not. All we can cling to is that even though we do not know why God does what He does, we can know that nothing thwarts His purpose, and that in all things He works for our good.[5]

Never Let Go of God's Love

The second step in the upward cycle to emotional success is to love or, more precisely, to remain in God's love so that His joy may be in you and that your joy may be complete.[6]

To trust God means to be enveloped by His love. And as we remain in that love, we are able to love others and avoid slipping into the self-centeredness of the negative downward cycle of emotional failure.

Love is a choice—a decision. No one is forced to love anyone, and God was not forced to love us. He had a choice from the very beginning. He could have decided not to love, and I have a feeling the thought crossed His mind more than

61

once throughout the history of the human race. But over and over again God remained who He was—love itself. In love He gave, in love He continues to give.

And in love we can respond. Because God decided to love each of us, we have a choice. He gives us the freedom to love or not to love; He did not create us to be robots.

I often hear questions like these:

"Why is there evil in this world?"

"Why do bad things have to happen—especially to good people?"

"If God is such a great God and is so omnipotent, loving, and kind, why does He allow evil to take place?"

"Why does He allow hate?"

"If God is so good, why isn't everything perfect?"

I don't have the answers to all these questions—I don't believe anybody does. But I do believe it all boils down to one thing. We all have a choice. God loved us enough to create us with a free will. He does not force us to love Him— or to love anyone else. Many people choose not to love, and out of that comes horrible evil. But if God had created all of us to be robots, with no ability to think or feel, we would have no real capacity to love because love is a choice.

So we live in a tension. As long as we have free will, there will be evil because there will always be those who, for one reason or another, decide not to love. As long as we are free to make decisions of our own, the world will not become a perfectly happy place.

*L*ove
is
a
choice.

—————◆—————

Is There a Way to "Live Happily Ever After?"

Happiness is the most sought after and illusive emotion on this planet. There are many, in fact, who would equate success with "being happy."

Harold Kushner is a rabbi who gained best-seller fame with his book *When Bad Things Happen to Good People.* Later, however, Kushner wrote what I believe is an even better book entitled *When All You've Ever Wanted Isn't Enough,* which he describes as not being about how to be happy or popular. According to Kushner, *When All you Ever Wanted Isn't Enough* is a book about how to be successful, but not in the way most people use the word.[7]

Most Americans are familiar with the Declaration of Independence and its guarantee of everyone's right to the pursuit of happiness. Kushner says, however, that "pursuing happiness" is really the wrong goal. He writes:

> You don't become happy by pursuing happiness. You become happy by living a life that means something. The happiest people you know are probably not the richest or most famous, probably not the ones who work hardest at being happy by reading the articles and buying the books and latching onto the latest fads. I suspect the happiest people you know are the ones who work at being kind, helpful and reliable, and happiness sneaks into their lives while they are busy doing those things.[8]

The reason Kushner is right is because of words uttered by another rabbi two thousand years ago:

> . . . remain in my love. If you obey my commands, you will remain in my love, just as I have obeyed my

Father's commands and remain in his love. I have told you this so that my joy may be in you and that your joy may be complete. My command is this: Love each other as I have loved you.[9]

Rejoice in the Lord—All the Time

The third step in the upward cycle of emotional success is to rejoice. First you trust God, knowing that He is in control and that all He does is done well. Resting on that trust, you remain in His love, obeying His command to love, not because you have to but because you *want* to. And the result of that is what Jesus called "complete joy."

Like love, joy is a decision. Sometimes the circumstances aren't very happy ones. We can know pain, disaster, frustration, anger, rejection, despair. But always we have the choice to believe or not to believe, to trust or to doubt, to thank God and rejoice in what He has given us or to turn away from Him.

When the Apostle Paul wrote to a church in an obscure place called Philippi, he told the believers there to "rejoice in the Lord always." Not once in a while, but always, no matter what the circumstances.

Why did Paul say that? Because life had always gone well for him and his theme song was a first-century version of "Let the Good Times Roll"? Hardly. Many people do not realize that Paul wrote these words about rejoicing from a prison cell, chained to a Roman guard, while awaiting possible execution.

That execution eventually did happen, but I'm sure Paul died rejoicing anyway. Paul understood that God and His ways are a mystery far beyond us. We never know what God is going to do in order to fulfill the desires of our hearts.

Things that may seem like devastation and disaster at the time can often be the doors to success.

Rejoice! Everything Is Smashed!

There is a story about a young architect who dreamed of getting the contract to build a beautiful new office building for a large corporation. He met with many of the executives from the corporation individually and discussed everything that they wanted in this building. Then he went back and poured all of his time, talent, and most of his bank account into constructing a beautiful model of the building they wanted.

This is often the way architects go about their tasks—first putting together a model so everyone can actually see what the building will look like and how it will function, and then drawing up the actual plans for the real thing. These models often turn out to be very expensive, and the architect spent just about everything he had to get the model ready for a presentation to the executives of the corporation. And at this point he still didn't have the contract. He was hoping that his bid would be accepted as the best one.

Holding the model carefully in his hands, the architect got on the elevator to go to the top floor where the executives were waiting in a board meeting. But as he got off the elevator, he didn't notice that it had stopped just an inch or so below the floor and he caught his toe and tripped. He fell right on top of his model, reducing it to shambles.

The young architect was devastated and then, as he was gathering up the pieces, someone came out and said, "The officers of the corporation are waiting for you to present your building."

The young architect didn't know what to do but he decided he had to keep going. Carrying the pieces and parts of the building in his hands, he stepped into the board room to be greeted by a large group of high-salaried executives who were sitting around a beautifully carved circular table, over which hung a chandelier as large as the table itself.

Still speechless, the architect put the pieces of his model on the table and waited to be laughed at and dismissed.

Instead, however, the executives looked at the pieces and one finally said, "Well, *this* is a brilliant idea."

"It . . . it is?" the architect stammered.

"Yes, of course—we love this idea."

Then one man got up, came over to the pile of pieces and parts, and picked one of them up, saying, "Ah, here's that tower I hoped the building would have. I bet it goes right here, doesn't it?"

Next the chairman of the board came over and picked up some other pieces, saying, "Hmmm . . . this looks like my big corner office. Perfect!"

Then others gathered around, picking up the parts and pieces and putting them all in the right places. Soon the entire model was reconstructed and everything fit exactly as the board members had pictured it would.

The young architect got the bid. Disaster had turned into success.

Rejoicing Can Save Your Life

The story of the architect's smashed model is obviously apocryphal, but it makes a telling point. Even in disastrous circumstances, you can see the bright side and rejoice. No one I know of reflected this truth more fully than the Apostle Paul, whose life was filled with one obstacle and persecution after another. Nonetheless, Paul could rejoice in the most dismal situation, and one of his letters is known as

"The Epistle of Joy." In this tiny book, known as the Letter to the Philippians in the New Testament, Paul begins by saying, "I always pray with joy. . . ."[10]

How can you and I *always* pray with joy? That is an interesting question, and I learned something about the answer early in my ministry, when I had to make hospital calls and sit at the bedside of people who were as far from joy as anyone could possibly be. Many of these people were in a coma and quite possibly never heard a word I was saying.

I remember going to see one patient who was lying on his bed, unable to talk. Tubes were coming out of his arms, and from everywhere else it seemed. He was obviously on the verge of death.

I was still an intern and had little or no training in how to deal with this kind of situation. I thought to myself, *What in the world can I possibly say for this poor man?* I touched his arm gently, looked at him for a few seconds, and left. I didn't know what else to do.

Three weeks later my father asked me to go on a hospital call with him. We walked into that *same* hospital room, and there was a different man in almost the same condition. Tubes were coming out of everywhere, and all he could do was moan softly.

Before we entered the room, my father said, "Robert, let me show you something. John may not be able to hear a word I say. I don't know whether he can or can't, but I am going to believe he can."

As we moved closer to the bed, my father said,

"John, how are you doing? This is Robert Schuller. You don't have to answer me. I know you can hear me. I know your mind is clear and you understand every word I say. You're a little weak right now. You've gone through a lot and you're weak and you can't talk. I know that, and don't worry about it. It's okay.

"Do you know what? You've got the best doctors in the world. You're in the best hospital. You're going to make it. You're not going to be in this pain much longer. God is with you, John. Let's have a prayer.

"O God, thank You for John. Thank You for His life, thank You for his family. Thank You for the doctors. Thank You for this hospital. O God, have John regain his strength quickly. We believe—we know it's going to happen. Thank You, Lord. Amen."

Then my father did a strange thing—at least it seemed strange to me. He gently grabbed John by the cheeks, put his face very close to his, and said, "John, I love you. We'll see you later." Then we left that hospital room.

When we had walked in, there had been no joy whatsoever, but with my father's prayer, joy had entered that room.

I learned later that the first man—the one I had gone to see—had passed away shortly after I had been there. But the second man—the one my father had prayed for—pulled through and is alive today. Is it possible that praying joyfully can make a real difference? Obviously, it is not some magic cure-all, because we cannot manipulate prayer and God in such a fashion. But I learned something that day from my father. I learned that anyone can pray joyfully if he will just *look for the positive*. Take a moment to look at all the good things that are happening, and you will always be able to pray with joy.

You see, joy is not a state of "being anything." *Joy is a decision*. We tend to say if this would happen or that would happen, then we could have joy. But joy doesn't depend on having a job, being married, being single, or being anything else. Joy is not dependent on your state of being; it is de-

When you're down with a frown turn your dial and put on a smile.

---

pendent on your state of consciousness. Joy is a conscious decision that we make.

There in that hospital room as my father prayed, I was reminded of another truth he taught the family as I was growing up. Every day, before my four sisters and I left for school, my father would have us repeat these lines from Ella Wheeler Wilcox:

> *I'm going to be happy today,*
> *Though the skies may be cloudy or gray.*
> *No matter what comes my way,*
> *I'm going to be happy today.*

My father taught us that the brain is like a radio. "You have to turn your dial," he'd say to me when I came down to breakfast with a sad or grumpy face. "Robert, stop right now and turn your dial."

Whether skies are sunny or gray, turn your dial to trust, love, and rejoicing. *That* is how to stay on the positive upward cycle of emotional success.

Chapter 4
You Are What You Eat—And Then Some

To this point, we have looked at three critical areas in which we develop cycles of success or failure: the spiritual, the mental, and the emotional. There is a fourth critical area, however, that many people often neglect—the physical. Let me warn you that I'm gong to be saying some things that may challenge your present life-style, particularly what you are eating. If I happen to offend you, please understand it isn't intentional. I'm only trying to help you develop success cycles regarding that most precious of possessions—your health.

I have been blessed with good health for most of my life. Throughout my childhood I rarely missed a day at school because of illness. To this day—I'm now thirty-five—I have never spent a night in the hospital or had to deal with any major physical injury or disability.

I believe there are several reasons for this long run of good health, the most important of which are God's graciousness and "good genes."

The Schullers have always been a rather healthy lot. I think especially of my Uncle Henry, who lived to be ninety-three. In his later years, he was in full-time ministry at the Crystal Cathedral, ministering to senior adults. The day before Uncle Henry died, he was preparing Sunday school lessons and making hospital calls.

Because of my general physical history and heritage, I was always under the impression that I was a specimen of "good health." I looked upon health food enthusiasts as a bit extreme, if not "nutty." During high school, college, throughout my twenties, and into my thirties, I ate pretty much what I wanted. When I wished to indulge in junk food, I'd justify it by saying, "I'm in good shape, I lift weights—what's the harm in a cheeseburger and a batch of french fries for dinner?"

In February 1988 all that changed. I was thirty-three at the time and my wife, Donna, who has always been very health conscious, challenged me to get my cholesterol level checked. I agreed to do so, confident that I was sound in mind, body, and spirit, and any tests that I could take would only confirm just how healthy I really was.

When the results of my test came back, however, I was a little surprised. My cholesterol level was 208, approximately eight points above the recommended maximum. I decided that the laboratory had made a mistake and six weeks later I took the test again, just to prove to Donna that my only problem was that I had eaten too many eggs the day before I took the first test. Whatever I wanted to prove to her, in the back of my mind, I wanted her to be sure there was absolutely *nothing* wrong with my diet.

When the results came back the second time, my score was 218! Now I was really chagrined, and it didn't help any when Donna pointed out that 10 percent of the American population have blood cholesterol levels that place them at "severe risk" of heart attack.[1] I knew enough about high cholesterol levels at the time to realize that if I didn't change my life-style, I probably wouldn't live to be ninety-three like my Uncle Henry, who had been among other things a missionary to China, serving God throughout his entire adult life with strength and vitality.

I paid a visit to my local bookstore to see what they had on cholesterol and what I could do to create a healthier me. The clerk directed me to a book entitled *Controlling Your Cholesterol,* by Dr. Kenneth Cooper, director of the Cooper Clinic in Dallas, Texas, and author of several best-selling books on aerobics.[2]

I spent the next week devouring that book as if I were going to have a final exam on it that would determine my future. In fact, that is exactly what happened. Dr. Cooper's book caused me to make changes that dramatically impact the way I live today. Not only did the book help me understand what cholesterol actually is and how to control my cholesterol level through diet, but it also gave me valuable tips on how to develop and maintain cardiovascular health.

Since then, Donna and I have continued to study physical fitness and have read numerous books and articles in order to create healthier bodies with which to serve God for as long as He desires.

We have identified the negative health cycles that plague millions of Americans as well as the positive health cycles that can give anyone more energy, better health, and stronger resistance to disease, fatigue, and stress. First, let's look at an all too familiar problem for millions of Americans.

The Negative Cycle Begins With Temptation

The negative health cycle (*see* Figure 8) begins when we are tempted by media hype, delectable sights, and cultural

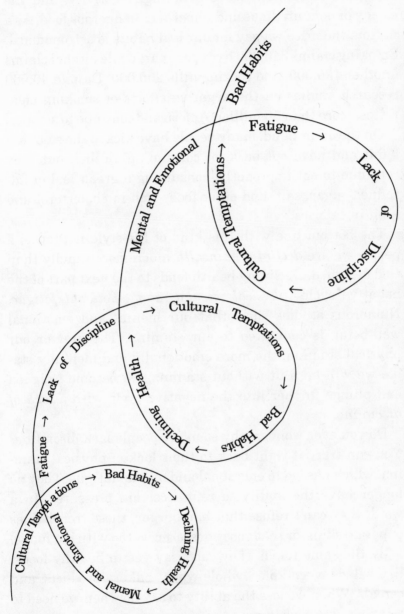

Figure 8: The Negative Downward Cycle to Poor Health and Early Death

delights. All these enticements lead to *bad habits* which include smoking, excessive drinking, inactivity, and the eating of nonnutritious and sometimes dangerous food. As a nation, the price we pay for our bad habits is astronomical. Smoking claims 346,000 lives per year, while alcohol claims another 125,000, and cocaine kills 200,000. Despite 40,000 research studies on the negative effects of smoking cigarettes, more than 50 million Americans continue to smoke.[3]

On the other hand, many people have kicked the smoking habit and have cut back on consuming alcohol, but they continue to eat improperly, consuming a great deal of fat, refined sugar, salt, and other foods rich in cholesterol and high in calories.

The bottom line with this kind of life-style is that as a people we are *declining in health* much more rapidly than God designed. Declining health leads to the next part of the negative cycle—*physical, mental, and emotional fatigue.* Numerous studies show that our mental and emotional well-being is connected to our stamina. The greater our physical stamina, the more emotionally and mentally stable we will be. But without stamina, we become fatigued and plunge further into the negative cycle with a *lack of discipline.*

Do you ever wonder why so many people lack discipline? You can trace it right back to their lack of physical stamina, which has led to emotional and mental fatigue. They no longer have the ability to refuse certain pressures. In a word, they can't refuse that hamburger, those french fries or potato skins, or that gooey dessert covered with hot fudge.

By the same token, they can't say yes to healthy foods, like salads, vegetables, whole wheat bakery products, and cereals. When we lose the ability to say no when we need to say no and yes when we need to say yes, the impact on our lives can be enormous. Not only is our physical health affected, but so is our spiritual well-being.

The Apostle Paul struck a good balance between the importance of the physical and the spiritual when he told his young protégé Timothy: "Take time and trouble to keep yourself spiritually fit. Bodily fitness has a certain value, but spiritual fitness is essential, both for this present life and for the life to come."[4] From personal experience, I know that I am stronger spiritually when I am eating right, exercising properly, and saying no to all that tasty but very bad stuff that is being advertised twenty-four hours a day.

Negative Health Is a Downhill Treadmill

As the negative health cycle continues, our lack of discipline leads us to more bad habits, which lead us to further declining health. We find ourselves mentally and emotionally fatigued, and finally, we slip into an even greater lack of discipline. Soon we are on a treadmill headed downhill, which can only lead to an early death.

It need not be. God has designed us to live a long and healthy life. According to His plan, human beings should live to an average age of 120.[5]

According to the government statistics, we are dying in our 70s when we should be living to our 120s. The chart below lists life expectancy at different ages.[6]

If you are now . . .	Your life expectancy at birth was . . .	
	Men	*Women*
25	72.7	80.6
45	70.4	77.9
65	64.1	71.9
85	54.0	61.4

Obviously, average life spans are being dragged down considerably by people who kill themselves with tobacco, alcohol, and drugs, but don't forget the effect of diet on how long you can live. In his book *Fats and Oils,* Udo Erasmus discusses the good news and bad news concerning high-fat diets for children.

In the seventeenth century, the average age for a girl's first menstrual period was around seventeen years old and her diet contained 20 percent fat. Today a girl has her first menstrual period at thirteen, on a diet containing 42 percent fat.[7]

Not only does a high-fat diet speed up the onset of puberty, it also increases growth rate and adult body size. In other words, children on a high-fat diet get bigger and taller. You may have seen news items on how we have grown taller and larger over the last hundred years. One big answer is a diet much higher in fat.

Have you wondered why the Japanese are much shorter than Americans? Their diet contains less than 15 percent fat, while ours has over 40 percent. What happens when Japanese people move to the United States and start eating Western style? According to Erasmus, ". . . their children become taller, and the same phenomenon holds true for other racial groups around the world."[8]

While fats help people mature earlier and grow taller, the bad news is that people who live their entire lives on high-fat diets burn out quicker. In other words, they age more quickly and die younger. There are very complex theories about why this is true, but the bottom line is that if you want to live longer, *cut your fat intake.*

The Positive Cycle for Good Health

The Bible's teaching that man is designed to live to 120 is confirmed by scientists who admit we are genetically programmed to live beyond 100, but because of our life-style and environment, few of us make it to that age. The more I studied the negative health cycle which decreases life span, the more it was relatively simple to come up with a positive health cycle that would increase it (*see* Figure 9).

When you get on a roll with the positive health cycle, the cultural delights that bombard you from every direction will not have their same lure and power. As you learn proper ways to eat and live, you create *right habits* and a new life-style, which develop a *healthier body*. This, in turn, creates *mental and emotional strength* as a by-product. And this mental and emotional strength gives you the ability to develop *stronger discipline* to do what you need to do to create the proper habits that will give you the longevity that God designed you to have.

Not only do we want to live as long as God designed us to live, but also we have the responsibility to live in a way that glorifies Him and which acknowledges that our bodies are His temple.[9]

Because the folly in using tobacco, alcohol, and drugs is self-evident, I want to focus on the proper diet that can lead to a positive health cycle. If you are not convinced by the results of all the studies that have been done on the dangers of tobacco and drugs, I doubt that anything I can say here would have much effect. I can, however, give you some thoughts about how you might change your diet habits in the interest of better health. I hope what I say will not sound like a "crusade against junk food." Actually, you could never darken the door of a junk food restaurant and eat what you considered to be very nutritious food and still be consuming far too much fat, refined sugar, and salt.

As I mentioned, my interest in proper diet began when I scored too high on cholesterol tests and read Kenneth Cooper's book *Controlling Your Cholesterol*. As I have continued reading other material on this subject, the answer to lowering cholesterol and increasing cardiovascular health has become plain: *Avoid foods that are high in fat, refined*

Figure 9: The Positive Upward Cycle to Good Health and Longer Life

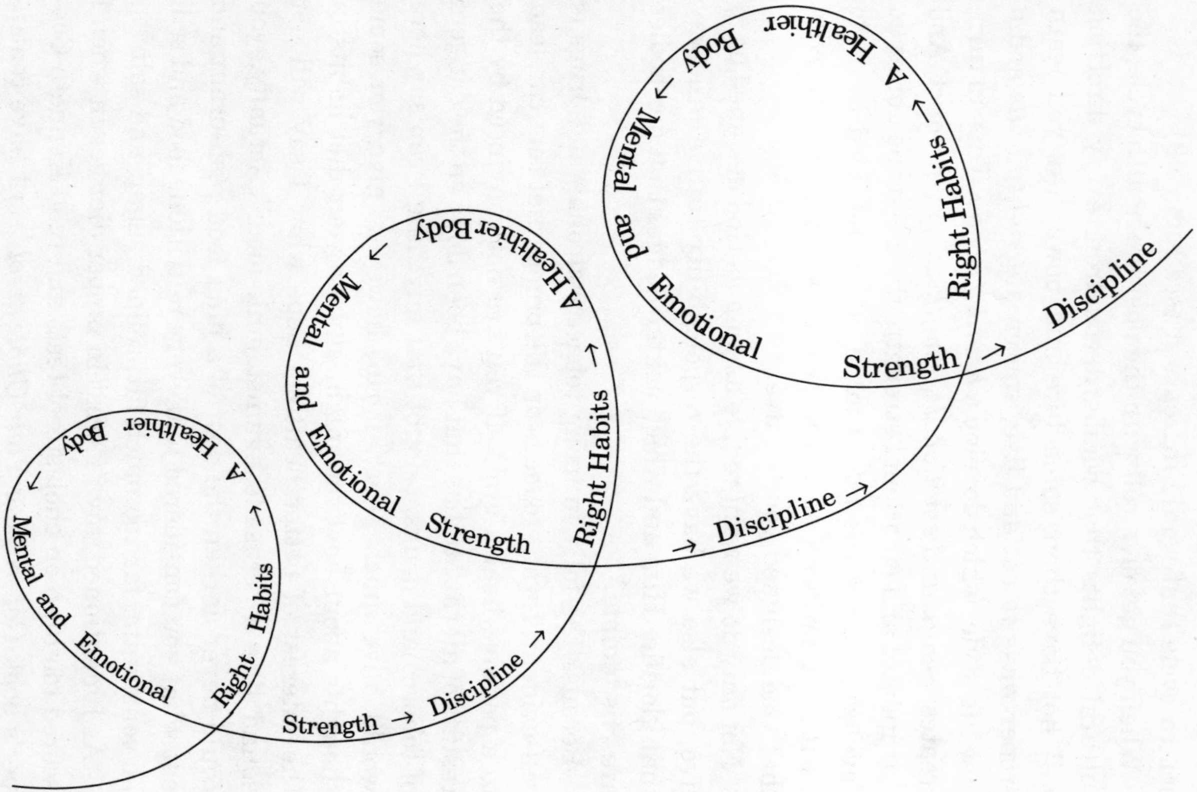

Discipline → Strength → A Healthier Body → Mental and Emotional → Right Habits → Discipline

Discipline → Strength → A Healthier Body → Mental and Emotional → Right Habits → Discipline

Discipline → Strength → A Healthier Body → Mental and Emotional → Right Habits *sugars, and salt.* And if you want to zero in on the most dangerous of these three villains, avoid fats whenever possible.

Actually, avoid all *processed* fat whenever possible. At Kenneth Cooper's aerobics center in Dallas, they recommend that your diet be made up of 50 percent complex carbohydrates, 20 percent protein, and 30 percent fats. Cooper writes:

> Whether you want to lose weight or maintain your present poundage, this 50-20-30 percent distribution of three food types is the most fundamental principle for establishing the proper equilibrium. . . .[10]

Your body needs some fat, but try to stay away from the unnatural kinds that are processed. Olive oil, safflower oil, and corn oil (which are often advertised as "healthy") are to be avoided whenever possible. In addition, avoid butter, margarine, and cheese.

Not surprisingly, people with weight problems do not avoid fat—in fact, they eat too much of it. Quite possibly, the "battle of the bulge" is the longest running war ever fought, particularly by Americans. In 1989, Americans spent $33 billion on diet and diet-related products.[11]

A chief reason for all this dieting is that too many people eat processed foods that are high in fat. In a typical meal, 75 percent of the calories consumed can be fat, and yet people often think they are eating "healthy"!

In short, most people who have a weight problem eat a large amount of fatty foods. When it comes to playing the dieting game, the domino effect is definitely present. Lots of fatty foods means too many calories. To reverse the domino process, however, avoid fat and you will keep your calorie count (and your weight) down.

Today there are all kinds of diet centers, weight loss programs, and diet clubs that all charge a lot of money to teach you to do one thing—eat healthy and consume fewer grams of fat. Many of these businesses sell their own packaged foods, prepared without oils, and, of course, everything is low in fat.

Follow the rules and regimens of these organizations, eat what they tell you to, and they guarantee that you will lose weight. Of course you will lose weight! All you are doing is controlling the amount of fat grams that go into your body. To paraphrase one diet/exercise expert, the best way to keep fat out of your arteries and off your frame is by *keeping it out of your mouth.*[12]

It may be helpful to some to be a part of a club or have the counseling of a diet center, but if you're serious about cutting down on your consumption of fat, you can easily do it yourself. You can lose the weight and save a lot of money.

How Much Fat Is Permissible?

According to statistics, the average American diet reportedly consists of 42 percent fat. The recommended goal is 30 percent or less, but that is not always easy to achieve. In her informative little booklet *Thirty % Fat . . . What's That?,* Patricia Ormsby Borer points out that a lot of high-fat foods are cleverly packaged and marketed to conceal just how much fat is really there. She writes,

> Since fat itself has little or no taste, it is masked with other "goodies." In reality, what is presented as "heavenly melt in your mouth" is "deadly delight!"[13]

Is there a simple way to have your diet contain 30 percent fat or preferably even less? Yes there is, if you are willing to do a little simple arithmetic and become aware of how many fat grams there are in various kinds of food. Because men and women have different calorie requirements per day, let's look at women first to see how it works.

According to most diet and nutrition specialists, a 1,500-calorie diet provides the average minimum daily requirements for any woman who wants to maintain her present weight. If such a woman wants to maintain the recommended percentages of 50 percent of complex carbohydrates, 20 percent protein, and 30 percent fat, those 1,500 calories have to be divided as follows:

Complex carbohydrates — 750 calories
Protein — 300 calories
Fat — 450 calories

So far, so good. But how can we help this woman count the grams of fat it will take to amount to 450 calories? We need one piece of information: Every gram of fat contains 9 calories. If we are attempting to eat no more than 450 calories of fat per day, that means we must divide 450 by 9, that is, $450 \div 9 = 50$ grams of fat per day.

What about men? According to the diet specialists, the average minimum calorie requirements for a man who wants to maintain a stable weight is 2,200 calories per day.[14] Using our same formula, that means that he must divide his calories among the three basic food types as follows:

Complex Carbohydrates — 1,100 calories
Protein — 440 calories
Fat — 660 calories

At 9 calories per gram of fat that means that a man trying to maintain his weight by consuming no more than

2,200 calories a day can eat around 73 grams of fat per day—660 ÷ 9 = 73.

If you want to keep track of how many grams of fat you are eating per day, you must obtain any one of several excellent books that list the number of grams in typical servings of basic foods and food dishes that most people eat daily. One book I particularly like is *Eat to Succeed* by Dr. Robert Haas.[15] I have based my figures here on Dr. Haas's figures.

I use myself as an example to show you what can happen if you don't notice or care about how many grams of fat you are eating daily. I'll give you examples of some typical meals that I used to eat before getting my "cholesterol wake-up call" in 1988. As you will see, I was consuming almost unbelievable quantities of fat, that were far in excess of 30 percent of my total diet.

No Wonder My Cholesterol Was Too High

One of my typical breakfasts was two fried eggs, which contain almost 14 grams of fat. To that I'd add at least three slices of bacon, which would total at least 12 more grams. Two slices of toast have very little fat, but when I added a tablespoon of butter (12.2 grams fat) to each slice that would give me another 24.4 grams of fat.

I liked whole milk and would often drink an eight-ounce glass, which added another 8 grams. On many mornings I'd match the bacon and eggs with a good serving of hash browns—another 12 grams of fat. I used to drink cream with my coffee, and, at around 3 grams of fat per tablespoon of coffee cream, that could add anywhere from another 5 to 10 grams of fat, depending on how much coffee I drank.

Roughly speaking, then, for breakfast on some days, I could easily put away at least 81 grams of fat!

Let's not even talk about having a coffee break (with more cream) and adding a big roll with at least one or two tablespoons of butter at 12.2 grams per tablespoon. Let's move on to lunch, for which I would typically head for McDonald's. I ate lunch at McDonald's several times a week, and my usual menu was a Big Mac (31 grams of fat), an order of fries (around 13 grams of fat), and a chocolate shake, which, strangely enough, contained "only" 8.5 grams. My guess is the chocolate shake is not too high in fat grams because McDonald's makes their shakes with low-cal ice cream and nonfat milk to keep the cost down.

At any rate, for lunch, then, I would add another 52.5 grams of fat, and I still had dinner ahead of me!

Again, let's just skip afternoon coffee break—where it would be easy enough to have any number of fatty treats—and sit down to dinner. Suppose I started with spareribs (which I dearly loved). A healthy serving of spareribs runs around 38 grams of fat. If I put at least a tablespoon of butter on my vegetables, which I was prone to do, that added another 12.2 grams of fat.

Of course, I had a salad and always felt that I needed at least two tablespoons of salad dressing. Two tablespoons of blue cheese dressing gave me a good 15.5 more grams of fat.

The common potato has no fat to begin with, but I would add one tablespoon of butter (12.2 grams of fat) and several tablespoons of sour cream (2.5 grams of fat per tablespoon), for at least another 10 grams. For dessert I might go "lightly" and have just one scoop of fairly rich ice cream, which would be almost 12 grams.

Dinner, then, gave me another 99.9 grams of fat, and my grand total for the day was an astounding 233.4 grams, *over three times the recommended amount!*

I realize that you may not eat anywhere near this much

each day, but this example of how I used to eat gives you an idea of how important the counting of fat grams is. For example, if you frequent the fast-food restaurants at all, be aware of just a few startling numbers:

One McDonald's apple pie = 18.3 grams fat
One Taco Bell beef burrito = 21 grams fat
One Colonel Sanders Kentucky Fried Chicken thigh = 19 grams fat
One McDonald's Egg McMuffin = 20 grams fat
One McDonald's Quarter Pounder with cheese = 28.6 grams fat

As you can see, some real villains in the fat gram battle are butter (12.2 grams per tablespoon), cream (anywhere from 3 to 5 grams per tablespoon, depending on how rich it is), salad dressing (around 8 grams per tablespoon for any of the usual dressings like blue cheese, french, russian, or thousand island), and cheese (9.4 grams per ounce of cheddar).

How I Lost the Desire for Fatty Foods

The incredibly fatty diet I described above is not even remotely close to the kind of diet I consume today. Even though I could allow myself 70 to 80 grams of fat per day to stay well within the 30 percent range, I prefer to shoot for 30 grams or less, in order to maintain even better health.

Because I know a McDonald's Big Mac has over 31 grams of fat, I have not had one in the past two years. In fact, *I have not eaten a hamburger in the past two years.* When I started my new low-fat diet in 1988, hamburgers still tempted me. After all, I was hooked on Big Macs. But as I got stronger in my discipline, the cravings for Big Macs, and any kind of hamburger for that matter, went away. Eventually, I lost the desire for hamburgers completely. Today they don't even tempt me at all because I know how loaded with fat they are and how harmful they are to my health.

Perhaps you are wondering how to develop the discipline to stay away from the fatty favorites you're used to eating. Here are some suggestions that have worked for Donna and me:

• Avoid using all oils. Instead follow the "four *B*'s"—bake, broil, boil, or barbecue your foods.

• Avoid frying whenever possible. If you need to fry foods, simply coat the pan with a little cooking oil spray.

• Don't put butter on your bread. Don't add cheese to your sandwich or other foods.

• Avoid most prepackaged and fast foods.

• Avoid salad dressings. Donna and I enjoy seasoned vinegars and nonfat salad dressings. There are many different products on the market now.

• Drink nonfat milk. Nonfat milk has the same number of vitamins and minerals as whole or low-fat milk, but none of the fat.

• Instead of eating ice cream, try nonfat frozen yogurt or nonfat ice milk. Both are great in our opinion!

Donna and I love pizza, and we eat it regularly. In fact, we consider it to be one of our major healthy foods. How can that be? Isn't pizza considered junk food, and, besides, isn't it loaded with cheese? You're absolutely right, but we order only "no-cheese pizza."

Next time you're feeling adventurous, try ordering pizza

without cheese. I won't guarantee that that's what will come back from the kitchen. Sometimes the cooks just don't believe what is written on the order! Donna and I have gotten many a free pizza for our children, which was made with cheese by mistake. Now we usually go to certain pizza parlors where we're recognized the minute we come through the door. Then we get what we want—a large pizza with *absolutely no cheese and no butter.* For toppings, we order anchovies, onions, bell peppers, mushrooms, and uncooked tomatoes. We never order any pepperoni or other meat toppings.

A lot of people doubt whether they would like no-cheese pizza, but try it. It has a tremendous amount of flavor and is very low in fat, and you can eat the entire thing because the bloated feeling you get from cheese and oily meat is not there.

How to Eat 30 Grams a Day—and Less

Perhaps you're wondering what kind of food I eat today—on a low- or no-fat diet. You may think that I'm starving myself and have to eat like a bird. Not so. To be honest, I still eat *very substantial meals.* The only difference is that now I keep my count of fat grams well below a total of 30 for the entire day. This is how I do it.

For breakfast I might have my favorite—pancakes. Yes, I said *pancakes*—something that usually conjures up images of lots of calories and fat in the minds of most people. You can run up a lot of grams of fat with pancakes, but the kind I make come out around 1 gram of fat per four- or five-inch cake.

I use a mix that I get at the health food store, or sometimes I buy a "light" mix at the supermarket, both of which are practically fat-free. I add nonfat milk, along with applesauce, bananas, and sometimes blueberries or some other fruit for extra flavor.

Because I love pancakes, I'll have as many as ten for breakfast and my total number of fat grams consumed will be right around 10 grams. With the pancakes I will have some light syrup, of course, which is high in calories but contains no fat. I also have a bowl of fruit and a glass of nonfat milk (no fat in either one), and I drink my coffee black (no cream, thank you).

With 10 grams of fat consumed so far, I head for lunch, and again, I hardly go hungry. I often have two turkey sandwiches, which are made with no butter or mayonnaise. I use two slices of bread per sandwich and pile on generous amounts of turkey, mustard, lettuce, tomatoes, and salad peppers. Total amount of fat grams consumed is approximately 9 (5 grams for the turkey and another 4 grams for the four slices of bread).

Because I love Donna's low-fat muffins, I often nibble on a couple of those as well, not worrying about fat because each muffin contains only .5 grams (see recipe, p. 98). For dessert I might throw in a scoop of frozen nonfat yogurt, which contains a little less than 2 grams of fat per four-ounce serving. My total for lunch, then, is somewhere around 10 or 11 grams of fat.

For dinner I will have vegetables with no butter, which means no fat. On my salad I put a fat-free dressing. Many recipes are available for making your own or you can buy some excellent brands in the stores.

For our main dish, Donna often fixes Chicken Curry, a magnificent (and almost fat-free) dish, which includes chicken breasts, all kinds of delicious spices, and brown rice (see recipe, p. 99). It comes out at 1.3 grams of fat per serving, and I usually have at least three helpings. We got the Chicken Curry recipe out of another excellent book by Dr. Robert Haas, *Eat to Win*.[16] Another favorite dinner dish

Donna often fixes from Dr. Haas's book is Chik 'n' Chili, which has only 1.9 grams of fat per serving (*see* recipe, p. 100.)

For dessert I love Entenmann's fat-free chocolate cake and some fat-free ice cream, which you can find in most grocery stores. Dinner, then, costs me in fat consumption less than 5 grams.

For the day, we see that I have consumed approximately 25 or 26 grams of fat, and yet I have had ample, and in some cases, huge, amounts of food. My weight seldom varies more than two or three pounds; I have tremendous energy and enjoy superb health in general. Fat-free eating really pays!

What About Too Much Sugar and Salt?

Another real villain in the typical American diet and in much of the processed food that we may buy is sugar. Not only is it exceptionally high in calories, but excessive sugar can cause your blood sugar level to swing dangerously high and low.

Your best bet is to train your taste buds to enjoy the flavors of whole natural foods as God created them. Natural flavors are often lost through processing, as manufacturers continue to sell consumers on the thought, "If it isn't sweet, it isn't good."

If you're trying to cut down on sugar, watch the carbonated soft drinks. They contain enormous amounts of sugar, and it would be far better to drink water, nonfat milk, and 100 percent *pure* (not "natural") fruit juice. And of these three, your best bet by far is water.

Besides fats and sugar, you should watch your intake of salt. The dangers of a high-salt diet are well-known to people suffering from heart problems and high blood pressure. Donna and I have discovered that it is far better to allow our foods to render forth their own flavors. Various spices can give you all kinds of flavors to enhance any meal, and many of the spices available on the market today do not contain salt.

Also, never salt your foods as you are cooking them. In fact, avoid salting food whenever possible. Avoid all processed foods; they are automatically high in salt (not to mention sugar and fat—usually all three are present).

Donna and I use a lot of fresh garlic, and we grow several of our own herbs, including sweet basil, mint, and thyme. We've found these plants easy to grow and we don't need to use any space in our backyard. We grow our spices in pots in the kitchen window and have more than enough all year around. It's well worth the little bit of trouble because the flavor we get from homegrown spices far surpasses what we can buy in stores.

Healthy Eating Is Only Half the Answer

Eating right is only part of staying fit. The other half of the positive health cycle is exercise.

Unfortunately, one of the worst habits Americans have is inactivity. As a country, we prefer to sit in front of the TV set and nibble on snack food, rather than get out and go for a walk, a run, a swim, or a bike ride. This sitting and snacking is a great way to develop all kinds of cardiovascular problems and our physical health will decline much more rapidly than God ever designed.

The fact is, God designed our bodies for exercise. When we don't get any, we are destroying that design and hastening the aging process as well as encouraging a negative health cycle. Whether we eat too much or don't exercise enough, the ancient truth of the Scriptures always reminds us that we reap what we sow.[17]

Healthy eating
is only half
the answer.

———— ◆ ————

Motivation Has to Come From Within

I can't motivate you to exercise. That has to come from within. My own story about getting motivated to exercise goes back to when I was fourteen and a sophomore in high school. At the beginning of fall term, we were given forms on which we could sign up for various sports and other activities. Wrestling caught my eye. I'd wrestled with my dad at home, and I felt skilled in that area. Surely wrestling would be a great after-school sport that I could participate in throughout high school.

I reported to the gym along with five hundred other students, eager to get started. The head of the P.E. department gave us all a pep talk and then he read off the names of students who had signed up for various sports. I'll never forget what happened when he called off my name to go to the wrestling room.

"Robert Schuller—wrestling," he said loudly. There was a brief silence, and then it seemed as if all five hundred guys started laughing and hooting at me. I was so humiliated and embarrassed that I left the gym and went straight home. I never reported for wrestling during my sophomore year.

Why had everyone laughed when they heard Schuller wanted to wrestle? Because at the time I was shaped like a pear, not a wrestler. I had narrow shoulders, a small chest, and a large waist and hips. Yes, I was a fairly big kid compared to most of the other boys in the school, but it was distributed in all the wrong places!

Not long after my wrestling debacle, I was in the high school weight room with a few of my friends, most of whom were much smaller than I was. We began playing around and trying to lift some of the weights. One of my smaller friends picked up a forty-five-pound barbell and, with tremendous effort, managed to get it over his head.

All the rest of my friends lifted it, too, and then they turned to me and said, "Okay, Robert, your turn!"

Since I was bigger than any of them, I stepped forward with confidence. This couldn't be too difficult. I quickly lifted the barbell up to my chest and began to raise it above my head. I was surprised to learn that it would go only as high as my nose. With incredible effort I managed to get it level with my forehead, but I could not straighten my arms out and press the weight to its full height above my head.

My friends were polite and didn't laugh at me too much, but I was humiliated. It was at that point that I decided I needed to do something about my physical condition. It was then that the desire to exercise "came from within."

The very next semester I enrolled in a weight-lifting class. I still couldn't press forty-five pounds above my head when I started, but my instructor taught me to begin with weights I *could* press and build my body from there. For two years weight lifting was my selected physical education course for credit as well as my constant after-school pastime.

When I began my senior year, I had a much different physique from the one that had been laughed out of the gym when I was a sophomore. No longer was I shaped like a pear. My shoulders and my chest were developed, and my waist and hips were trim. Now I could bench press nearly three hundred pounds. And that forty-five-pound barbell I couldn't even lift above my head with two hands two years earlier? Now I could easily lift it above my head with one hand several times.

Because weight lifting had given me a new physique, it had also given me new self-confidence. I signed up for the wrestling team and did well. That year I was named "most improved wrestler" and also took third place in the Southern California tournament finals.

I Thought I Was Really in Shape Until . . .

After graduating from high school, I continued to use various exercises to stay in shape, including running, racquetball, and some weight lifting. Throughout my twenties and into my mid-thirties, I thought I was in fairly good shape. But, in December of 1988, not long after I had those cholesterol tests, a friend of mine gave me a gift of a free body-fat test from his personal trainer. Because I was tall and had a slim, muscular build, I felt I would pass that test with flying colors. I knew that a desirable fat content for a man is 15 percent of body weight, while women are allowed 22 percent because they aren't as muscular. I was sure I'd be well under the male limit—*maybe around 10 percent,* I thought smugly.

When I got the results, I was surprised to learn that my "lean" body actually contained 16.5 percent fat. That really wasn't bad compared with the standard for men, but I was really chagrined when Donna took the same test and her body fat was only 14.5 percent, compared with the standard of 22 percent for women.

Once again, motivation to exercise "came from within," and I immediately started a new exercise program that I'm still following. It features stationary bike riding, "stair-stepping," and weight lifting. If you have read anything having to do with the "fitness craze" of the last decade or more, you have probably run across the term *aerobics.* For good cardiovascular fitness, you need to engage in at least three sessions of aerobic exercise every week, each session lasting for at least fifteen to twenty minutes. Of course, before beginning any exercise program you should always consult your doctor.

When you exercise aerobically, your goal is to get your heart rate up to at least 70 to 80 percent of maximum, and continue steadily in whatever you're doing for a minimum of twelve minutes. Many fitness books recommend running and jogging, as well as walking, cycling, swimming, stair climbing, and skipping rope.

When it comes to exercise, "to each his own." Donna and I prefer our stationary bike and our stair-stepper machine, which get us to 70 or 80 percent of our maximum heart rate with no trouble at all. I am not in favor of running or jogging, because of the wear and tear it causes on one's entire system, particularly the legs, knees, ankles, and feet. I am also not enthusiastic about outdoor bicycling because of the obvious dangers involved.

How to Compute Your Aerobic Level

You may be wondering how you compute 70 or 80 percent of your maximum heart rate. The formula is simple and I'll use myself as an example:

I start with 220 and subtract my age. That gives me my maximum heart rate of 185. Let's say that I am shooting for 75 percent of this in order to engage in aerobic exercise, 75 percent of 185 is 139. That means I must get my heart rate up to at least 139 beats a minute in order to say that I am engaging in aerobics.

In order to know if my heartbeat is at least 139 beats per minute, I need to take my pulse. The experts differ on how to do this. Some suggest counting heartbeats for six seconds and multiplying by ten. Others suggest counting for fifteen seconds and multiplying by four. Dr. Kenneth Cooper recommends fifteen-second counts, monitoring the pulse at the wrist or by placing the hand over the heart. He does not recommend taking the pulse at the neck because pressing on the carotid artery can actually slow the heart down and not give you a true picture.[18]

Donna and I don't do aerobic walking, but I highly recommend it. Walking has come into its own in the last few years, and it has opened up all kinds of possibilities to many people who felt that running or other more strenuous exercises were just out of the question.

While Donna and I engage in aerobic exercises like stationary biking and stair-stepping, our personal all-around preference for exercise is weight training. It's the best way to increase muscle tone and work on all the major muscle groups of the body. And, the more muscular you are, the more calories you will burn naturally.

While most fitness books will not list weight lifting as an aerobic exercise, Donna and I lift weights in series of quick repetitions with very little rest in between, and we always obtain a good aerobic effect.

I realize that many people would not be interested in weight lifting. Walking might be much more to their taste, and that's great. The important thing is to exercise *regularly*— at least three days a week to maintain fitness. According to Covert Bailey, author of the best-selling fitness book *Fit or Fat?*, you lose fitness if you exercise two days a week or less. You maintain it if you exercise at least three days a week for a minimum of fifteen to twenty minutes each, and you improve fitness if you exercise six days a week.[19]

No Instant Answers on Fitness

Obviously, there is much more that could be said about how to eat and exercise correctly to maintain a positive health cycle. In this chapter I have touched on a few major points, but if you grasp their importance, you are well on the way to cycles of fitness success. Remember:

1. *Eat less fat.* Limit your total intake to 30 percent of

your total diet each day and, for even better health, stay under 30 grams of fat per day, which would be well under 30 percent of your total diet.

2. *Do aerobic exercise regularly*—at least three times a week. Nintendo or walking the dog don't count.

If you ignore these two simple but basic rules, you are bound to stay on a negative downward cycle to poor health. You will continue gaining weight, trying to diet, losing a few pounds, then regaining those pounds plus a few more. And keep in mind that every time you diet and later regain the weight, your body becomes more loaded with fat than ever.

Only *you* can make the decision to change your lifestyle—not just for a seven-day diet or a six-week program, but *for life*. Some of those changes will be difficult. Donna and I both know that. Giving up things like Big Macs, cheese, and nuts, for example, was no fun at all. But now we have fuller, richer lives and actually eat all we want without gaining weight. You can do it, too, and have the rich, fulfilling life that God intended.

APRICOT BANANA MUFFINS
(Donna's own recipe)

1½ cups whole wheat pastry flour
½ cup bran
½ cup granulated fructose
1 cup chopped dried apricots
2 bananas, mashed
1 tablespoon baking powder
1 cup applesauce
2 egg whites
½ cup skimmed milk

Preheat oven to 350 degrees. Spray muffin tin with PAM. Mix all ingredients except skim milk and eggs in a large bowl. Lightly beat egg whites. Gradually add milk while beating and fold into rest of mixture. Fill muffin tins two-thirds full. Bake 25 to 30 minutes or until wooden tooth-pick inserted in center comes out clean.

NUTRITIONAL INFO PER SERVING:

Calories 105
Protein .... 1.8 g.
Sodium .... 10 mg.
Carbohydrates .... 25.1 g.
Fat .... 0.3 g.
Cholesterol .... 0+ mg.

CHICKEN CURRY
Serves 4

8 ounces chicken breast, cubed
Pepper
¼ teaspoon cinnamon
1 tablespoon Tamari soy sauce
¾ cup onion, finely chopped
½ cup celery, chopped
1 teaspoon garlic, minced
1½ tablespoons curry powder

1 bay leaf
1½ cups apples, cubed
⅔ cup banana, finely diced
2 teaspoons tomato paste
1¾ cups chicken broth, defatted
½ cup evaporated skim milk
½ cup raisins
4 cups cooked brown rice

1. Sprinkle chicken cubes with pepper.
2. Place ¼ cup chicken broth and Tamari in a large saucepan. Add chicken and brown.
3. Add onion, celery, and garlic. Cook briefly.

Sprinkle with curry powder. Add rest of ingredients except apples and evaporated skim milk.

4. Cover and cook 10 minutes. Add apples and cook 5 more minutes.
5. Add evaporated skim milk. Heat through.
6. Serve over beds of brown rice.

NUTRITIONAL INFORMATION PER SERVING

Calories	*434.2*	*Carbohydrate*	*83.0 g*
Protein	*22.7 g*	*Fat*	*1.3 g*
Sodium	*1008.2 mg*	*Cholesterol*	*51.7mg*

CHIK 'N' CHILI
Serves 6

6-ounce can tomato paste
¼ cup onion, chopped
¼ cup wine vinegar
¼ cup Worcestershire sauce
1 teaspoon dry mustard
4 cloves garlic, minced
2 tablespoons Parmesan
   cheese

2 tablespoons granulated
   fructose
½ cup skim milk
½ cup breast of chicken,
   cooked and cubed
1 cup corn
16-ounce can Heinz
   Vegetarian Beans, rinsed

1. Combine all ingredients in large saucepan.
2. Simmer 30 minutes.

NUTRITIONAL INFORMATION PER SERVING

Calories	*179.1*	*Carbohydrate*	*32.7 g*
Protein	*9.2 g*	*Fat*	*1.9 g*
Sodium	*503.3 mg*	*Cholesterol*	*11.1 mg*

The recipes for Chicken Curry and Chik 'n' Chili are from Dr. Robert Haas's *Eat to Win*, pp. 276, 277.

Chapter 5
Your Home—A Haven of Peace?

by Donna Schuller

Every woman, I believe, wants her home to be a haven of peace. No matter what kind of pressures bombard my family from the outside, it's my goal to keep our home a place where my family can enjoy freedom from strife and feel secure, loved, content, and calm.

While I subscribe to this beautiful ideal wholeheartedly, I realize making peace happen is another matter, especially when you have children ranging from two and a half to twelve years. At our house, at least, there are times when it seems all too easy for "war" to break out. Instead of tranquility and serenity, I find myself right in the middle of squabbles that can turn into minor and, in some cases, major storms.

Often, I'm right in the eye of the storm myself. My ideals and goals for a haven of peace mock me, and I find myself on the edge of slipping into a failure cycle. Instead of peace, I

This chapter is based on a Mother's Day message presented by Mrs. Robert A. Schuller, Rancho Capistrano Community Church, May 9, 1987.

101

feel guilt, anger, and disappointment at not being able to live up to my values and ideals.

There are all kinds of enemies who would make war on the peace in our homes. We live in a society that bombards us daily, particularly through television and other media, with all kinds of traps, temptations, and dangers. But I believe one of the most deadly enemies we face comes not from the outside but from within. As that well-known theologian Pogo said, "We have met the enemy and they is us!"

How are we ourselves a threat to peace in our homes? Let me illustrate by telling a story related to me by a friend who has small children of her own. She'd had a very busy week and had not seen her children very much. As my friend was getting out of the shower one day, her three-year-old daughter came into the bathroom and gave her a big hug. "Mommy, I love you," the little girl said.

My friend's immediate response was, "Well, Honey, I love you, too."

Then the little girl hugged her mother even tighter and said, "Mommy, I wish I had a mommy just like you."

Out of the mouths of babes who speak with no hidden agenda can come striking truths! My friend admitted to me that the little girl's remark, spoken without guile or rancor, had made her think about her overly busy schedule. She realized that she had been having sitters and other child-care services substitute for her presence far too often in the past few months. She had to admit that the hug from her daughter reminded her that their hugs had been all too few as of late.

"My daughter's remark made me take a step back and realize that I hadn't been home that much," my friend told me. "I'd been racing around with all these outside activities, and what I needed to do was start focusing more on what was really important in my life."

I thanked my friend for telling me her story and then I

went off and took a little personal inventory of myself. My friend wasn't the only one who had been doing a lot of running around lately and who hadn't been focusing on what was really important. The truth hit me—hard. "Being busy," often with very laudable, worthwhile projects, can be a deadly enemy of peace in your home. Squabbles, fights, and wars can start when you neglect being there to talk and pray with, answer questions, give hugs, cookies, kisses—whatever else might be needed at the moment.

How to Make Peace at Home

Most families are familiar with how war can start at home, but how do we make peace when we *are* there? One simple approach that I have found very helpful is to simply use the word *peace* as an acrostic:

> <u>P</u>atience
> <u>E</u>ncouragement
> <u>A</u>cceptance
> <u>C</u>orrection
> <u>E</u>mbracing

Seen from this perspective, the word *PEACE* can become a ladder that you and your family can climb on the upward cycle of success (*see* Figure 10). Each step is a key to making and keeping peace in your home.

All Parents Need Patience—Now

Patience is something all parents want—and most of us preferably want it right now. Because "right now" is when we need it—when little Jimmy claws at our leg and screams while we're trying to get dinner ready, or when little Lisa refuses to go to bed and wails for a drink.

I confess that I qualify as a likely candidate for the "Lord, give me patience and give it to me now" syndrome. Robert and I were married in November 1984 and about six weeks after we returned from our honeymoon, his three-year-old son and six-year-old daughter moved in with us. Immediately my childhood expectations of what it would be like to be a wife and mother underwent some alterations! I had been a "career woman" used to being independent, on my own, and not having to deal with the feelings and desires of other people. In any new marriage, the husband and wife have to adjust to each other, but I had an "instant family" to adjust to as well!

During those first months and years of our marriage, I leaned on a verse from the Old Testament a great deal:

> But those who wait on the Lord
> Shall renew their strength;
> They shall mount up with wings like eagles,
> They shall run and not be weary,
> They shall walk and not faint.[1]

I had always liked that verse, maybe because I spent several years as a flight attendant with Continental Airlines. The idea of waiting on the Lord and then "mounting up with wings" appealed to me. But when I got married, I often found myself grounded for one reason or another.

I wondered what had happened to the room-service menus, uninterrupted hot baths, and just reading the newspaper. And one of the most frustrating things for me was reconciling my perfectionistic "a place for everything and everything in its place" approach to housekeeping with the much more casual approach of my stepchildren.

One thing that actually helped me was that Robert and I

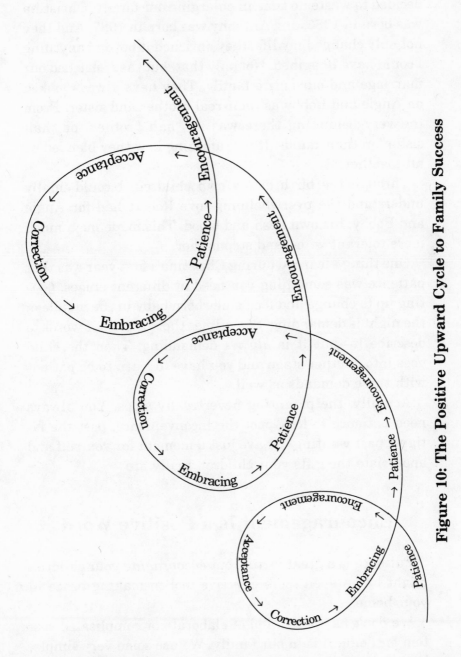

Figure 10: The Positive Upward Cycle to Family Success

decided to waste no time in enlarging our family. Christina was born in 1986, and Anthony was born in 1987. And they not only changed my life, they enriched it beyond anything I could have imagined. Not only that, but they enriched our marriage and our entire family. They have always looked on Angie and Bobby as their real brother and sister. From the very beginning there was no "half brother" or "half sister" in their minds. It was amazing how they blended us all together.

Through the birth of my own children, I could finally understand the overwhelming love Robert had for Angie and Bobby, his own flesh and blood. This made me a much more tolerant wife—and stepmother.

One thing I learned during Christina's first year was that patience was something you need at different stages. Getting up to change and feed a newborn baby in the middle of the night is demanding. Sometimes there are other words to describe it—but it is *always* demanding. Then the child goes into another stage and you have to learn to be patient with those demands as well.

Actually, the parenting never really stops. You always need patience to look past the inconvenience, past the fatigue, past wanting to have just a moment for yourself and appreciate the gifts your children really are.

Encouragement Is a Positive Word

Patience is a great virtue, but *encouraging* your children might be an even more effective tool in making peace in your home.

We don't have any kind of elaborate or complicated system for doing this in our family. We use some very simple, basic means of positive reinforcement, and they work for us. Whenever our children earn awards or certificates, we buy a frame and put that sign of recognition up on the wall of their room, or possibly it goes on display in our kitchen.

It might be a dentist's certificate saying, "Good work, keep on brushing!" Or it might be an award earned at their school. When Angie and Bobby were in Harold Ambuehl Elementary School in San Juan Capistrano, they earned "golden eagle" coupons for outstanding schoolwork or for good behavior. When they accumulated ten golden eagles, they qualified for special recognition—lunch out with the principal and a beautiful certificate from him as well. Several of these awards hang on our walls proudly, recognizing and encouraging the children's behavior and achievement.

To some parents this might sound like overdoing it a bit, but we don't think so. Whenever the kids walk into their rooms, or even flick on the light at night, they see those awards hanging on the wall and it reminds them, "Hey, you're all right. You've done things that people have recognized—you're doing okay."

I know this is what I felt when I was a child and I would go to the "star chart" my parents had on the wall for me. They had all the standard things up there—go to bed on time, brush your teeth, pick up your toys. There were many more—I can't remember them all now. And every time I did one of those things, up would go a star. By the end of the week, or perhaps it was the end of the month, I got a special toy, a special meal, an ice-cream cone, or something else when my star chart was all filled in.

While stars and awards are good, one of the best forms of encouragement is simply verbal—reminding kids that you think a lot of them and that you are behind them. The greatest verbal encourager I can think of is Jesus Himself. To *encourage* means to "put courage into," and He was constantly doing that for His disciples and those whom He helped.

To the paralytic, He said, ". . . Son, be of good cheer; your sins are forgiven you."[2] When His disciples' boat was tossed about by the storm and they feared drowning, Jesus came to them walking on the sea, saying, "Be of good cheer! It is I; do not be afraid."[3]

In just these two instances you can see a pattern in Jesus' encouragement. He encourages His disciples to *cheer up* and *not be afraid*. That's the bottom line concerning what your children need. They do have fears; they have anxieties; they have worries. They need constant reminders that all will be well, that Mom and Dad love them, and so does God.

Acceptance Means Forgiving Seventy Times Seven

There is a lot of talk today about *acceptance*, especially "unconditional acceptance" of those close to you. To unconditionally accept your children and spouse is a great ideal and goal at which to aim. Doing it is another matter! When I think of accepting my children, I'm especially reminded of the power of genetics.

In recent years, articles have appeared, reporting that scientists are discovering that genetics and heredity have a much greater influence on a person's personality and behavior than do upbringing or social pressures. According to one report, "The debate over what has been called 'nature versus nurture' seems to be taking a decisive turn."[4]

Studies of hundreds of sets of twins, including forty-four pairs of identical twins, show that how people think and act is determined more by their genes than by environment or parental influence. Studies have also shown that genetics help explain tendencies toward being an alcoholic, suffering severe depression, or fighting weight all your life. "The research bolsters what parents have always sensed: even within a single family, each child right from birth is different."[5]

This profound "discovery" by researchers is not news to most parents who have more than one child. We are all aware that our children are vastly different, but the point is, they bring these differences to the family *from birth*. What parents must remember is to accept who their children are instead of rejecting them for having a certain temperament or characteristic.

When Bobby was five and a half, one of the things I had to learn to accept was the simple fact that he could not remember what we would tell him to do for the next five minutes. We would be getting ready to go somewhere, for example, and practically everybody would be in the car— everybody except Bobby. "Bobby," I'd say, "run up and get your shoes on, okay? We'll all be waiting in the car for you."

Five minutes later, no Bobby.

"Where's Bobby?" Robert would ask. "I wonder what happened?" Then either he or I would get out of the car, walk upstairs to Bobby's room, and there he'd be, reading a book or playing his record player.

"What are you doing, Bobby?"

"Oh, I don't know . . ."

"Well, don't you remember you were supposed to put your shoes on and get down to the car, and we're all leaving?"

"Oh, yeah . . . my shoes."

Unfortunately, this wasn't an isolated incident. He constantly would forget things he was told to do—sometimes in a matter of seconds. At first, it almost drove me crazy, but then I learned I had to understand that Bobby had been born with a certain temperament. Genetics have played a large part in determining his artistic, freewheeling nature. And now that he's older, his artistic qualities are getting to be quite an asset. During this past year, he finished third grade with a straight-*A* report card, as well as playing the lead in the school musical. In addition, he competed in Tae Kwon Do in the junior Olympics and won two bronze medals. And his school art project was chosen from among some four thousand entries for special recognition.

The point is, even if your child seems "hopeless" at one stage, hang in there. Let's face it: Because our kids do have certain personalities, there will be times when they "rub us the wrong way." Let's also face the fact that there are times when *we* rub *them* the wrong way! The key to peace in the home is to accept the child, not necessarily always excusing the behavior, but to work with the child and try to help him remember, as was the case with Bobby, or to cooperate, or whatever the problem might be.

There is a story I like in the New Testament about Peter coming to Jesus and wanting to know how many times he should forgive someone who had sinned against him. Was seven times enough?

Jesus said to Peter, "I do not say to you, up to seven times, but up to seventy times seven."[6]

What Jesus meant by "seventy times seven" was to forgive on an unlimited basis—*as often as it might be necessary*. And that's the key to acceptance in your home. Accepting your child when he or she is pleasing you and being "good," is easy. Accepting your child when your temperaments clash, or when his behavior is definitely below standards that you have set for your home, is extremely difficult. Acceptance has to be balanced by proper discipline.

There Is Always Room for Improvement

While it is obvious there are certain things about our children that we need to accept, it doesn't mean that we should let them develop any way they like. That would be deserting our responsibilities as parents. That's why the *C* in the P-E-A-C-E success cycle is so important in our family. *Correction* means taking action concerning negative or unacceptable behavior and making sure our children understand that their behavior is what we are concerned about—but that we still love them very much.

One of the best approaches to discipline we have discovered is what some child-rearing specialists call "logical" or "natural" consequences. We used logical consequences to help our daughter, Angie, who had an extremely bad habit of sleeping in and being late for school.

When Angie was nine, she simply could not make it to school on time, morning after morning. We bought her an alarm clock and helped her set it for 6:30 A.M. We scheduled breakfast for 7:00 and leaving the house for 7:40, so she could get so she could ride her bike the two short blocks to school and get there in plenty of time to be in class by 8:00 A.M. sharp.

Angie would get up somewhere between 6:30 and 7:00 on most mornings, but she often diddled in her room and then did not appear for breakfast. About 7:56 she'd dash breathlessly downstairs saying, "Dad, I'm going to be late, will you please drive me to school?"

And with those big eyes staring at him, what else could Dad do? "Sure, Angie, I'll drive you to school—hop in."

This went on for too many mornings, and I was getting very concerned. I discussed this with Robert, saying, "Angie's always needing a ride to school doesn't seem right. She's really developing some bad habits, and I think we're contributing to them by always giving in and making sure she gets to school on time. If she were ready by 7:40, she could ride her bike to school without any problem."

Robert agreed with me, and we worked out a plan to help Angie learn responsibility for getting to school on time. First we checked on all the things we were responsible for providing: her warm bed, her clothes, her alarm clock, help-ing her set the alarm clock, having breakfast on the table at a set time—this was our half of the deal. Angie's half was to be sure she got up, got herself ready, had breakfast, and was out the door in time to ride her bike to school and be in class by 8:00.

We explained all this to Angie, saying that she would definitely have to make a real effort to be on time because there might be a morning soon when "Daddy won't be avail-able to give you a ride." Angie didn't seem too worried. She agreed that it was a good idea and said she would try harder. For a few mornings she did, and then the same old behavior started again. One morning she came down and made her usual speech: "Dad, can I have a ride to school? I'm going to be late!"

This was the moment when the rubber would meet the road. What would Robert say? He replied, "Well, Angie, you know, I think this morning you should just go on to school and tell your teacher why you are late."

Angie looked at her dad in utter dismay—even with a little horror. "What do you mean I'm going to tell my teacher why I was late? You know I can't do that."

"Well, I'm afraid that's what you're going to have to do, Angie. I'm sorry, but we made it clear that you had to be responsible for getting up and getting to school on time."

After a lot of tears, Angie still had to pay the conse-quences. She had to ride her bike to school, arriving well after 8:00 A.M. All this was exceptionally hard on us. It's one thing to talk about setting up logical consequences, and it's another to enforce them!

But the pain we felt and the embarrassment Angie had to endure turned out to be well worth it. Having to explain to her teacher why she had been late changed Angie's behavior—almost overnight. She was never late after that, always out the door and on her bike by 7:40, with everything done: breakfast eaten, teeth brushed, bed made—even her homework was always ready!

Logical consequences may be painful, but they *do* work. I'm reminded of another verse from the New Testament which says, "No discipline seems pleasant at the time. . . . Later on, however, it produces a harvest of righteousness and peace for those who have been trained by it."[7]

Most Important of All—Hug Them!

Possibly the most important thing I can say about making peace in your home is that after you correct your children, you must *embrace* them. Hug them, tell them that you love them, and share with them the fact that God loves them as well. God forgives them for the past and so do you. Your words are important, yes, but your hugs are even more important.

A great deal of research has also been done on this whole area of touching and embracing. You may have heard that it takes eight hugs a day just to stay on an even, healthy keel. Psychologists have conducted numerous studies indicating that affection is a basic physical and psychological need that begins at birth and does not diminish as we grow older. When infants are not hugged, cuddled, and stroked, it is likely that they will not develop properly.

These "facts" gathered by scientists only confirm what most mothers have known and practiced since the beginning of time: Children need to be touched, loved, and embraced constantly. You can be patient and can encourage, you can accept and correct properly, but if you are not giving that all-important loving touch to your children, you will not have peace in your home.

The Downward Cycle Threatens Peace

Having looked at the positive upward cycle that builds peace in your home through patience, encouragement, acceptance, correction, and embracing, we need to take a close look at the negative counterparts that can bring discontent, fighting, and even war. The enemy of patience is *aggravation;* the enemies of encouragement are *criticism* and *disillusionment.* The enemy of acceptance is *conditional love* or little or no love at all; the enemy of proper discipline and correction is *neglect*; and the enemy of embracing and warm touching is *disregard* (*see* Figure 11).

Most parents start out the day vowing they will be patient with their children. Lurking just around the corner, however, is the possibility that in a thousand and one ways the parent can become aggravated with the child and lose patience.

Let's face it. Our kids know which buttons to push to aggravate us. At an early age (are they born with it?) they achieve the ability to know just how hard to push, just how loud to scream. And their ears become very sensitive to Mom and Dad's tone of voice. Most kids know when they're reaching the red danger zone just by how loudly their name is being uttered.

As I cope with the things my kids do through the day, I also cope with another basic challenge—trying to find time for myself. Some days, I find it extremely frustrating and feel that I'm always on call. I can't even have five minutes to take a shower. And as the interruptions pile up, it's easy to lose it. I start to raise my voice when I shouldn't. Then I start telling myself, it's not really the child's fault, it's me. I'm supposed to have control of this situation—at least that is what the experts tell me in their books. I have to admit I'm not always sure that's true, and when I get really aggravated, the child can be more in control than I am.

As the irritations erode your patience, you get to feeling that what you're doing isn't worthwhile. Parents don't get a lot of positive, immediate feedback or reinforcement. It

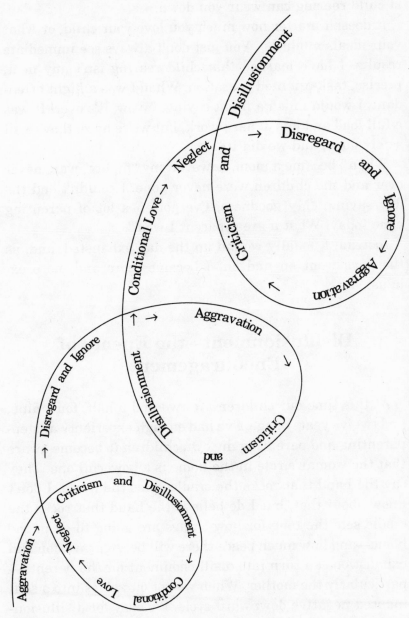

Figure 11: The Negative Downward Cycle to Family Failure

takes a long time to raise a child. The day-to-day doldrums of child rearing can wear you down.

It doesn't matter how much you love your child, or what your ideals might be. You just don't always see immediate results. I have learned that child rearing isn't any neat, precise, task-oriented operation. When I was a flight attendant, I would finish a flight saying, "Wow, it's over! It was a full load and lots of hard work, but we're here, they're all safely gone, and we did it!"

When I became a mom, however, my "flights" were never over and the children were never gone. I couldn't end the day saying, "My goodness, I've gotten a lot of parenting done today! What a great parent I was!"

Instead, I usually wound up the day exhausted, and, as the days went on and on, I became more and more exhausted.

Disillusionment—the Enemy of Encouragement

At this time our children are two and a half, four, nine, and twelve years of age. I've had enough experience at stepparenting and parenting my own children to become aware that the woman's role in the home is a powerful one. They say the hand that rocks the cradle rules the world. I don't know about that, but I do believe the hand that rocks the cradle sets the tone for how things are going to go in the home—and how much peace there will be. Aggravation and exhaustion can turn into disillusionment for the parents—particularly the mother. When we get ourselves into a self-induced negative downward cycle, it's easy for disillusionment to set in.

A couple of years ago I got tired of reading all the books by the experts telling me what I should be doing and then realizing I wasn't always pulling it off. My typical reaction was, "I'm not doing all this. I must be a lousy mom."

Realizing that I was being extremely self-critical and hard on myself, I started thinking about the other women in my church who had preschool-age children. I put out the word about starting a group Bible study and almost a dozen moms showed up at our first meeting. I said to the group:

"There are a lot of us here who are struggling with how to be better parents. We don't always feel that we are being the best that we can, but we don't have anybody to talk to about it. We may try to talk to our husbands when they come home from work, but they often have other things on their minds. Besides, they haven't been there all day with the children—they don't know what it's like. Their relationship to the children is different. They're not being pulled up and down, up and down, up and down on the roller coaster all day long the way we are. The typical dad comes home and it's all fun and games—'What's the matter?' he says. 'Why are you so uptight with the kids? They're great!' "

That opening speech sounded a familiar chord, and our first meeting turned into an honest sharing of feelings, frustrations, and needs. It went on from there, and we've met on every first and third Thursday morning each month for about two years now.

Our meetings start with about fifteen minutes of "catching up," social time, and prayer requests. Then, for the next hour and fifteen minutes or so, we have a very life-related Bible study. Right now we are working through a book called *A Mother's Legacy*, which provides studies of various mothers from the Old and New Testaments and the struggles they faced.

We come up with some very thought-provoking, relevant questions and discussions. The mothers always get help with their own situations—everything from how to get their children to take a nap, to potty training, to what is the best way to discipline? I like our group because we're structured, but not too structured. If our Bible study brings up a particularly important problem someone in our group may have, we stop and really share and help that mother with her problem.

Overall, our members have been extremely supportive of one another, and I believe that's one reason we have stayed together for over two years. It has been a real answer to prayer for all of us who fight disillusionment over our own lack of mothering skills. Twice a month we are living embodiments of encouragement to one another.

"Conditional Love"—Enemy of Acceptance

Every parent wants to accept his or her child and communicate genuine love no matter what the situation. But the deadliest enemy of acceptance is "conditional" love— "I'll love you *if* . . . " or "I'll love you *when* you perform this way." As I mentioned earlier, genetics can trip us up here because we do not understand our child's particular bent or temperament.

Many parents quote Proverbs 22:6, which says, "Train up a child in the way he should go, and when he is old he will not depart from it." They take that as God's promise to keep their children on the right path if they give them the right kind of upbringing. But from what I've been able to learn in Bible studies, this verse isn't talking about that as much as it's talking about training up a child *in the way God made him*, "according to his bent." In other words, if he is a musician or an artist, don't try to turn him into a halfback. If she loves bugs, the outdoors, and getting dirty, don't insist that she become a fashion designer.

You don't have to use the very words, "I'll love you *if*" to send a message of conditional love. Just go to any Little League game and you can usually find one or two fathers who are sending conditional love messages to their sons— especially when they strike out or miss the ball.

The message our kids need to hear in any setting is *"I love you no matter what*, no matter what you become, no matter what you want to do with your life, and no matter how you might mess up, *I'll still love you."*

As they open their excellent book, *The Blessing*, Gary Smalley and John Trent say this:

> All of us long to be accepted by others. While we may say out loud, "I don't care what other people say about me," on the inside we all yearn for intimacy and affection. This yearning is especially true in our relationship with our parents. Gaining or missing out on parental approval has a tremendous effect on us, even if it has been years since we have had any regular contact with them. In fact, what happens in our relationship with our parents can greatly affect all our present and future relationships.[8]

Neglect, the Enemy of Good Discipline

Properly correcting and disciplining children is a key to making peace in your home because fair, loving discipline throws up a wall of security and protection for the child. When children aren't properly corrected, they are usually insecure, and that's what leads to even more rebellion and misbehavior. Children need boundaries. They need limits and, if we fail to give them those limits, I believe we are neglecting them every bit as much as parents who are seldom home and don't even know what their children are doing.

In a sense, Robert and I were neglecting Angie when we allowed her to continue not being ready for school on time and then gave in when she begged her dad for a ride in the car. Finally, we threw up a boundary that said, "This is it, Angie, either you get up and be ready to leave on time, or you'll have to face the consequences at school."

Facing the consequences in real life is what correction is all about. If children aren't corrected while growing up, life and society have a way of correcting them, and it often can be a cruel shock. Many of the men and women serving time in our prisons could tell you that.

Have you ever had those days when it seems as if all you did was correct or discipline the kids? Every mother knows what I'm talking about. The children almost seem to become "the enemy." Their little antennas have a way of going up and they know just when to misbehave—especially if they feel you aren't giving them enough attention.

One of the common scenarios at our house happens when someone calls and I get on the phone. My children may have been perfectly content to that point with coloring or, perhaps, playing outside on the swing set. The minute the phone rings, they come screaming into the kitchen to scamper around my legs, wanting a drink, wanting a cracker, and just yelling like little Indians in general.

The two easiest courses of action are: (1) to scream, "BE QUIET!" or (2) to ignore all the din and try to talk on the phone anyway. A third possibility is to simply shoo them outside to play.

Instead, I need to say to the caller, "Excuse me." I need to put the phone down, take the children aside, and very quietly say, "Mommy's on the phone. When I get off the phone,

I'll be able to get what you want or play with you. Later we can have some fun together, but right now Mommy's on the phone and you're not supposed to interrupt. If you do interrupt, there will be consequences."

I seldom have to go beyond a quiet but firm speech along those lines. My children settle down and let me finish my telephone conversation, and then I try to make good on my promises to meet their needs or give them some time.

There are times, however, when they don't settle down, and then I have to say to the caller, "I'm sorry, I'm having some problems here and I'll have to call you back." Sometimes the caller may be irritated; he or she may even think that I can't "control my kids." On the contrary, I am deliberately taking time to try to control my kids and correct them in the best way I can.

Properly disciplining children and giving them loving correction is perhaps the most difficult task parents face. It's a lot easier to say, "Oh, it doesn't matter. I'll give you a ride to school," or, "Can't you see I'm on the phone? Get out of here and quit bothering me!" It is always tempting to take the easy, instant way out and not really bother to spend time communicating, explaining, and letting the child know that there are limits and these are the reasons why.

Parenting is a tough job and some parents fall into the trap of trying to buy their children's good behavior or love. They think that the more they do for their children, the better off their children will be and the better they will behave. To me, following that path never leads to peace, but only to bickering and misbehavior.

Ignoring Is the Enemy of TLC

If lack of correction equals neglect, lack of great quantities of loving and embracing your children can lead to the cruelest cut of all—ignoring them as human beings who need plenty of TLC, which I like to define as "Touch, Love, and Care."

Children's hospitals recognize the absolute importance of touch when they put children with serious illnesses in plastic bubbles or tents but always provide ways that the nurse or the parents can reach in with plastic mitts or gloves to touch and hug them.

As important as touching and caressing is for infants and small children, I believe the need continues as children grow older and become adults. Ultimately, we long for God's touch and loving care. The Psalmist asks God, "Keep me as the apple of Your eye; hide me under the shadow of Your wings."[9]

Time and again, the Gospels show us Jesus ministering with a healing touch. In many cases, people only had to touch the hem of His garment to become well.[10] Multitudes longed to touch Him and power would go out from Jesus to heal them all.[11]

Most important, perhaps, for parents is what Jesus said about the little children. Little children were brought to Christ so that He might touch them, but when His disciples rebuked those who brought them, Jesus said, "Let the little children come to Me, and do not forbid them. . . ."[12]

We live in such a sophisticated, verbal world that in many parts of the country touching and hugging are frowned upon. They aren't considered "dignified" or "proper." Obviously, there are times when this could be the case, but there are many more opportunities for people to hug and touch that are being passed by. The result is that children, and other adults particularly, are left feeling that they are being ignored, that no one really cares enough for them to touch them.

Every Mother's Day I get my Mom the standard card and gift, but I also take a moment to give her a very special

TLC
means Touch,
Love,
and Care.

"Thank You!" Now that I have children of my own, I recognize what a job she did in rearing me. I lost my father when I was thirteen, but she made up for it in so many ways. It was from my mother that I learned the importance of being patient, encouraging, and accepting. It was from her that I learned the fine balance between proper correction and always being willing to embrace and say, "I love you."

Many parents seem caught in the cycle of failure, or at least disappointment or discouragement, regarding their children. There is a way, however, to get on the cycle of success. It lies in parenting according to scriptural principles that have been around for thousands of years. The Bible is not a child-rearing manual, but it does give the basic principles we need to learn about how to be patient, encouraging, accepting, and loving in our correction and touching of our children each day.

As we trust in the Scriptures' timeless truths, we will "mount up with wings as eagles," because we have God's own promise: "My Word shall not return to Me void, but it shall accomplish what I please . . . believe according to My Word and you will live in joy—and peace."[13]

Chapter 6
Building Your
Network of Friends

One of the most insidious downward cycles in our present-day culture leads directly to a truly serious problem for millions of people—loneliness. I often ask myself, why are so many people lacking friends or even acquaintances with whom they can socialize? Why do millions of people complain of being lonely?

Sociologists describe some reasons why loneliness is more of a problem in our country today than it was a hundred years ago. For example, we have had radical changes in our morals and behavior, and we are also in a period when one in five Americans moves in any given year. People are constantly finding themselves "strangers in town," and making new friends is not an easy matter for many of them. Many have developed strong walls of defense because they have been hurt so many times from childhood on.

In his book *When You're Feeling Lonely*, Charles Durham starts his definition of *loneliness* by saying, "We might say that it is 'an empty feeling.' Yet it is obviously more complicated than that."[1]

Durham goes on to point out that loneliness is not the same thing as "being alone." Many people live alone and are quite content. Yet many other people live with a spouse and several children and feel very lonely. Loneliness occurs when inner needs aren't being met, when we don't feel understood, or when we feel as if our mate disapproves of us. And many have inner needs that were never met in childhood.

As he closes in on a definition, Durham writes,

> We can say that loneliness is pain caused by some sort of isolation from a person or persons. This isolation may be physical, ideological or emotional.[2]

Even in the Garden of Eden, God knew that loneliness is a real problem in man. He saw that Adam was missing something very important and said, "It is not good that man should be alone. . . ."[3] As John Milton put it, "Loneliness is the first thing which God's eye named not good."

How We Wind Up "Feelin' Lonely"

There are many reasons for feeling lonely. In my work as pastor and counselor, I often see a particular negative downward cycle that comes into play. One thing that I see is depending on oneself to the exclusion of anyone else. Another thing is an attempt to prove one's self-worth to others. Unfortunately, this only results in suffering wounded self-esteem and inevitably feeling lonely (*see* Figure 12).

The tendency to depend on ourselves is built into us from childhood. Most of us are taught to be strong, self-reliant, independent. These are all considered to be "good American values." Others learn that their worth is earned through trophies, compliments, prizes, awards, and so on.

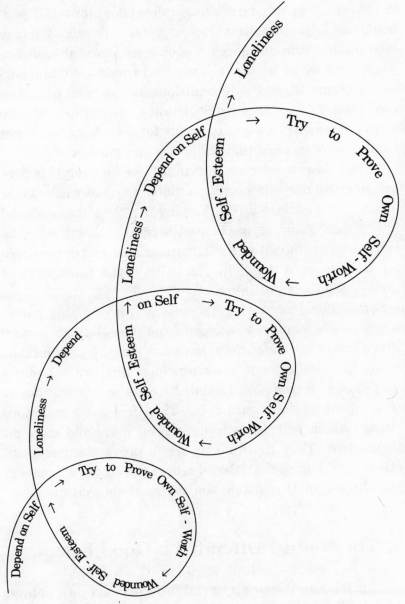

Figure 12: The Negative Downward Cycle to Loneliness

All these outward signs tell us and others that we are somebody.

This entire syndrome of being independent (or self-dependent) can be a stumbling block to making friends. We may have many "acquaintances"—people we know at school or work—but we do not have many real friends. We find ourselves trying to get the recognition that we need from surface relationships, not from genuine friendships. We are afraid to reveal ourselves to people for fear that they might think less of us once they know our weaknesses.

As the downward cycle continues, we do everything we can to prove our self-worth to others, many of whom know us only at a surface level. We play the "let's make a good impression" game, trying to use the right makeup, wear the right clothes, have the right mannerisms and speech. We try to be seen in the right places, have the right job, and always say the right thing.

Some people succeed quite well at playing this game. Many people seem very successful and "have lots of friends." Probe just below the surface, however, and you can find that many lack self-esteem, are suspicious, and are not really that close to anyone in particular. These people are caught in a repeating downward cycle. They feel more and more lonely, which only leads to depending more and more on themselves. They continue trying to prove themselves to others, and failing that, they discover that their self-esteem has slipped another notch. And so the cycle continues.

The Night I Offended a Good Friend

I recall going through a negative cycle of my own in high school. Like most teenagers, I was headstrong and independent. Concerned about being popular at school, I was always trying to prove my self-worth to others, particularly those in my own crowd. More often than not, however, I ended up with wounded self-esteem, feeling lonely.

One incident, forever branded on my memory, evolved around my wanting to go over and see my girl friend on a school night. To get out of the house, I told my parents I needed to go to the library to study. Impressed with my uncharacteristically studious attitude, my father gave me permission, saying that he was glad to see that I was "buckling down."

I left the house and did, indeed, go to the library, but only to drop off some books. Then I made a beeline to my girl friend's house.

Meanwhile, my father began thinking about what my motives might be for wanting to study so hard. Later in the evening he decided to call one of the people with whom I said I would be studying.

My father called my friend Cecil and asked him if he had seen me at the library. Cecil replied, "Robert? No I haven't seen him. Studying with him? No, I don't think so. The library? I doubt it."

When I got home around ten o'clock that night, my father met me in the front hallway with a cup of coffee in his hand. My mother collected teacups, and she had a wide selection and variety. She kept her precious cups in the china cabinet and ones of lesser value on a tea cart. Dad was allowed to use the cups from the tea cart.

He was sipping from one of the "not so precious" cups when I came in, and he seemed calm enough. "Well, Robert, where have you been?"

"Oh, I've been studying hard."

"Oh, really? Were you out with Cecil?"

"Yeah. We were quizzing each other really tough. It was a hard evening, and I think I'm ready to hit the sack."

There was a long pause as my father looked at me—hard. "Really . . . ," and then he smashed the teacup on the marble floor of the front hall. To say the cup flew into a thousand pieces would be an understatement. With anger blazing in his eyes, my father pointed at the broken cup and roared, "Robert, my trust in you is like that cup. That's how much water my trust in you will hold."

Then he walked away.

The downward cycle of being self-dependent and trying anything I could to build my self-esteem, even lying to my father, had cost me my friendship with him—at least temporarily.

The Fine Art of Having Friends

As we have seen in earlier chapters, for every downward cycle of failure, there is a counteracting upward cycle that can lead to success. This chapter isn't intended as an in-depth discussion of loneliness and how to deal with it. But I do want to focus on one specific way to avoid loneliness. Simply stated, we need to build a network of friends

When it comes to having friends, the positive upward cycle (*see* Figure 13) begins with *believing*. So often I hear someone tell another person, "I believe in you." I understand that they are trying to pay that person a compliment, but I believe the phrase suggests too much. To tell someone, "I believe in you," is to put your faith in a fallible human being who can disappoint you and even destroy your self-esteem. I suggest that a better approach is this:

BELIEVE IN GOD
AND LOVE PEOPLE

The purpose of this chapter is to suggest ways to build a solid network of real friends, but you don't build that network by trusting people to be more than they can be. We

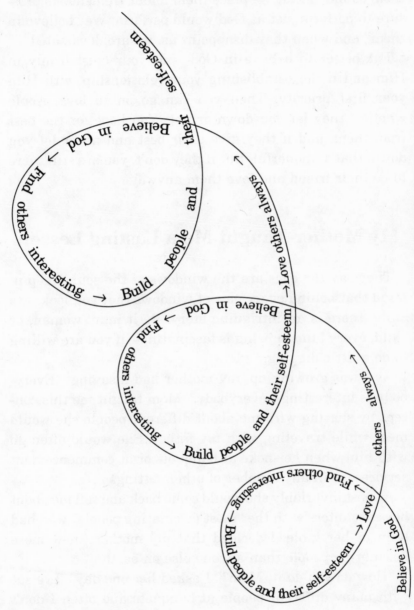

Figure 13: The Positive Upward Cycle to Lasting Friendships

often put so much stock in what people say and we count on them so much that we place them under tremendous pressure to perform just as God would perform. We "believe in them" and when they disappoint us, we are devastated.

Far better to believe in God—put your trust firmly in Him and make establishing your relationship with Him your first priority. Then you can go on to love people whether they let you down or not. You hope for the best from them, and if they give their best and never let you down, that's wonderful. But if they don't, you are still there to be their friend and love them anyway.

My Mother Taught Me a Lasting Lesson

They say the eyes are the windows of the soul. Keep in mind that behind every pair of windows that you look into daily, there is an intriguing story. Be it man, woman, or child, every human being is fascinating—if you are willing to do a little digging.

As I was growing up, my mother had a saying: "Everybody is interesting—everybody." Mom taught me this concept by sharing with me about different people she would meet while traveling with my father. She would often go with him when he spoke at banquets or at commencement services, or in any number of other settings.

Almost invariably she would come back and tell me about her encounters with the "most fascinating people" who had been at her table. I decided that my mother knew more fascinating people than anyone else on earth.

"How do you do it, Mom?" I asked her one day. "I've sat with many different people at banquets and often I don't know what to say."

"Well," she said with a smile, "I very rarely say much. I'm not a very good conversationalist. I just ask a question or

*E*verybody
is interesting—
everybody!

———◆———

two and then listen. You'd be amazed at the responses people give."

"What do you ask them?" I wanted to know.

"Oh, questions like 'Do you have a family?' or I might ask, 'Do you have any challenges?' That's an especially good one for people with young children, like two-year-olds. And then their hearts begin to open and the people begin to reveal who they are and what they really think about."

Ever since then, I took my mother's advice and became more interested in listening to people. I've found that she is right. Everyone *is* interesting. Everyone has a fascinating story or opinion.

Will Rogers is famous for saying, "I never met a person I didn't like." Jesus of Nazareth put it even better when He said, ". . . Love one another; as I have loved you . . . you also love one another."[4]

I realize you might be saying, "But I meet a lot of people I don't like. I'm not sure I can just learn to be interested in everyone." I'm not saying you have to suddenly become Will Rogers overnight. But I am saying that all of us can learn to reach out in friendly and understanding ways to more people, which can eventually lead to having more friends ourselves.

"Nice" Lessons for Angie

When my daughter, Angie, was around eight years old, she went through a stage of being very snobbish and stand-offish to just about everyone, even members of our church. She would be at a church function and people would come up and say, "Hello, Angie. How are you?" Angie's usual response would be to simply ignore them or give them a curt, cold answer.

After observing this behavior for ourselves on several

occasions, Donna and I took Angie aside for a talk. We told her she couldn't treat people that way, and we started giving her "nice" lessons to learn how to be a much nicer person. For example, we taught her how to respond when people came up and asked her, "How are you?" We taught her some of the fine points of being friendly and gracious— nothing complex or difficult, just plain, old-fashioned good manners and common sense.

It turned out that Angie wasn't as snobbish as she was afraid and unsure of herself. She was a willing pupil when we gave her "nice" lessons, and then one evening we put her to the test at a church potluck.

"Angie, we're taking you to the church potluck tonight, and you're going to have a chance to use the lessons we've given you on how to be nice," I told her.

As we drove to the church that evening, I wondered how Angie would respond. Would a few "nice" lessons make any difference? I didn't have to wait long to find out. We had barely gotten there when someone walked up to Angie and said, "Hi, aren't you Angie Schuller?"

"Oh, yes, I am," Angie responded graciously. "And what is your name?"

Then I heard someone else come up and tell Angie, "My, you look nice this evening. Is that a new dress?"

"Thank you," Angie responded. "I've had it for a while, but I'm glad you like it."

Throughout the evening Angie used everything we had taught her, and it appeared she had a wonderful time, but the best part came as we were driving home. Angie announced from the backseat, "You know, it's a lot more fun being nice. I'm going to be nice from now on!"

Nate Morrison: Nicest Man I Know

What my daughter Angie learned at the age of eight about being nice is based on the same principle we can all employ, no matter how old we are. One of the most fascinating people I've ever met is Nate Morrison, my associate pastor. Nate is in the Archery Hall of Fame. He has hunted big game with bow and arrow and competed successfully in many target tournaments as well.

But not only is Nate interesting, he's also nice—just about the nicest man I know.

Nate was watching the "Hour of Power" on television one Sunday morning when my father called me forward to tell the congregation that I would be leaving the Crystal Cathedral staff to start my own church somewhere in the San Juan Capistrano area. At that moment Nate felt a call from God to "go help that young man in his new ministry."

Nate had gone through the lay minister's training at Crystal Cathedral, and I had seen him occasionally. We would nod and say hello, but I didn't know him very well. About two weeks after that "Hour of Power" broadcast, Nate called me and told me that he had seen me announce my new church on television and that he had felt a strong call to assist me.

"Actually I put off calling you for about two weeks," Nate said. "At first I thought that it would be nice when you got the new church started and I would join. But God has distinctly told me that I am to help you, and if you can use me, I'll be glad to come aboard."

If I could use him! To that point, I had had very few offers of help. Nate had no idea what an incredible lift the sound of his voice gave me.

Nate came over to see me immediately, and we talked about the new church. He was with me from the ground up; we went through all the struggles together.

I will never forget the help Nate was on that Sunday morning in January 1984 when I had to announce to our congregation that I was getting a divorce. After the service,

I broke down and wept openly in the front of the church. Nate came up, put his arms around me, and told me that he loved me and that he was with me.

In the days that followed the divorce announcement, Nate seemed to know when to be there to talk and when I needed to be alone. He kept telling me, "All is not lost, Robert. You'll go on—we'll all go on with you."

Through the years, Nate Morrison has always been there. He is, quite simply, a real friend. Instead of wanting to build himself up, he always looks for ways to help me and build the church at the same time.

How to Make People Like You

So often I see people trying to win friends by working overtime on their own self-esteem, trying to build themselves up in the eyes of others. This almost always results in failure for a very basic reason: Most people aren't interested in you—they are interested in themselves!

Step number three in the upward cycle toward lasting friendship is to build up people and their self-esteem. Or, to put it more simply, make people feel good about themselves. Always be thinking of ways to help people understand that you love and care about them. Sigmund Freud said, "One of the greatest needs of any human being is the understanding of love and affection."

Another psychologist, William James, put it this way: "One of the greatest desires of any human being is to be appreciated."

But I like best of all what Lord Chesterfield told his son: "My son, here's the way to get people to like you. Make every person like himself just a little bit better, and I promise you that he will like you very much, indeed."

That line bears repeating. Do whatever you can to make

everyone you meet like himself just a little bit better, and that person will like you very, very much indeed. I have seen it happen again and again. If you can communicate to people that you really care about them, you will win friends every time. Build people up, give them a sense of self-worth and self-dignity and you will build lasting friendships.

Remember that it begins with placing your faith in God. Be grafted into the knowledge of His love and you will gain the spiritual humility that will build your own self-esteem and make you more capable of building others. Then you can reach out in love to others to help them understand the true beauty they have in their own souls.

The Monk Who Won Many Friends

There is a story about a Syrian monk named Telemachus, who lived in Asia Minor in the fourth century A.D. One day God said, "Telemachus, leave everything you have and travel immediately to Rome. I have need of you there." Telemachus obeyed. He grabbed his walking stick and set out for the great city of Rome, many miles away.

When Telemachus finally arrived in Rome, he found a city in the midst of rejoicing and festivities. The Emperor Honorius had just returned in triumph after conquering the Goths in the north.

In true Roman-conqueror style, Honorius had entered the city through the great triumphal arch, riding his massive white stallion. Behind him were prisoners in chains, taken in battle, now to be slaves.

A few days later, a time of massive celebration had begun. The emperor offered free admission for anyone wanting to come to the Colosseum to see the gladiators fight to the death. The Colosseum was packed—it seemed that everyone in Rome was there.

Telemachus was there, as well. And as he watched two gladiators come out and bow before Honorius and then draw their swords to fight to the death, Telemachus knew what God had called him to Rome to do. He squeezed through the crowd, got to the wall, and jumped down into the ring with the gladiators. Running between them, he stood there with hands outstretched, trying to stop their deadly duel. Telemachus shouted, "In the name of Jesus Christ, forbear!"

To hear the name of Jesus Christ shouted, even in the arena at the Colosseum, was not unusual. For the last four hundred years, the city had seen Christians. The city had seen the execution of Paul the Apostle. They had witnessed the martyrdom of hundreds, if not thousands, of Christians in that very arena. The soil on which Telemachus stood was saturated with the blood of past Christian martyrs.

But as Telemachus stood there, spoiling the "sport" many in the crowd had come to see, someone shouted, "Away with him!" The huge, well-muscled gladiators looked at the little monk with disdain. One gave him a shove, and he went rolling into the dust and hit the wall. But he bounced up again and ran back between their flashing swords, shouting again, "In the name of Jesus Christ, forbear!"

Again they pushed him to the ground and tried to go on with their battle, and again he prevented them from doing so.

Finally, the Emperor Honorius gave the signal. Without hesitation, one of the gladiators ran his sword completely through Telemachus. Then he pulled it out of the monk's quivering body, the blood dripping from the tip into the dust.

Telemachus sank to his knees and died in agony. As he lay there gasping for breath, a hush came over the stadium. Then one man, a member of the court of the emperor, stood up for all to see and walked out of the Colosseum. Never before had anyone ever dared to act with such defiance of the emperor's wishes.

Then, on the other side of the arena, from the crowd, another man stood up and led his family out. He was followed by still others and soon the trickle of people leaving became a stream, and then it became rivers of people flowing out of the Colosseum by the thousands.

Soon the stands around that bloody arena were practically empty, and never again were they filled by people who came to watch human beings battle each other to the death.

In Telemachus's dramatic sacrifice, you can see many inspiring truths portrayed, including the cycle of lasting friendships. Telemachus certainly believed in God and loved people. He obeyed God's command and journeyed all the way to Rome. Once there and in the Colosseum, he knew the task to which he had been called. He was to build people up, to show them that he loved them and that they must love one another.

I'm sure Telemachus never heard the term *self-esteem.* It wasn't part of the fourth-century vocabulary. But deep within his soul, he knew that people had to think more of themselves than to be willing to kill each other while thousands of their fellowmen sat around and watched in the name of "entertainment and sport." Yes, Telemachus died that day. His great love for people and for the worth of human beings cost him his life, but he won many lasting friends. And the example he set changed the course of Roman history.[5]

Putting Together a Shattered Frienship

The key to winning friends is to reach out in love and vulnerability, willing to be hurt, if necessary. I learned something about that on the night I lied to my father and watched him smash a teacup into a "thousand" pieces and tell me that his trust in me had been smashed as well.

After he stalked out and went to bed, I remained behind. I found a broom and a dustpan and swept up every piece of the teacup I could find. I put it all in a bag and took it to my room.

On the following day, I dumped all the pieces out on my desk, and one by one, I started gluing them together. It took hours to begin to match up the broken fragments. I spent over a week on my project, working at it whenever I had the chance. After approximately ten days, you could at least tell there was a cup where once there had been nothing but shattered fragments. You could see the glue marks all over the cup, and you could see holes where I wasn't able to find certain bits and pieces. Nonetheless, I had restored enough of the cup so it could hold water.

I took the cup and went to see my father.

"I want to apologize for what I've done," I told him. "I ask your forgiveness for lying to you and, most of all, I want you to trust me. I won't ever lie to you again."

Then I handed him the patched-up cup. He looked at it for a long moment, and I could see tears in his eyes. Then he hugged me and I knew our friendship was restored.

Today my mother still keeps her precious cups in the china cabinet and the less valuable ones on the tea cart. The cup I laboriously glued back together has a place of honor in the china cabinet. It is a lasting symbol of what it takes to make and keep a real friend.

Chapter 7
Harnessing the Power
of Money

It has been said that, for the typical person or family, the two most private things in life are sex and money. The unknown philosopher who made this observation is close to the truth. Furthermore, I'd say that of these two "forbidden subjects," which are to remain secret from the prying eyes of the world, money and one's financial style is the most sensitive of all.

Down through history, money has been a crucial part of life. In our society, particularly, there is little chance for people who have little or no money. For proof, you need look no farther than to the increasing number of homeless people who wander the streets and alleys of the land, sleeping under freeway overpasses in cardboard boxes or, if they are lucky, in threadbare tents in public camp grounds, moving on to somewhere else when their "camping permit" expires.

The sobering fact is that there are many other people who might not be called homeless but are still living at a poverty level and millions more having a terrible time just making ends meet. The days of husbands being breadwinners while wives remain at home to rear the children are a nostalgic anachronism. Today, the norm is that both parents have to work just to stay even in our consumer society. Recently, I heard a news report concerning a new bill in Congress regarding families. From that report came the statistic that in nine out of ten families both parents are employed outside of the home.

Everywhere you turn you can find people with tremendous financial needs. In over 50 percent of divorce cases, money problems are the major cause of marital discord.

We Spend Our Way Into Financial Trouble

We are well acquainted with the term *consumer society*. In America, life is built around getting people to consume more and more. Marketing has become an art form, as well as a much-coveted career by many college graduates. Philip Slater, whose book *The Pursuit of Loneliness* is an insightful critique of American culture, believes that the term *consumer society* should be taken in a literal sense. He writes:

> The advertising industry caters heavily to our growing need to be fed, while at the same time it aggravates it further by burdening us with more and more esoteric choices. . . .[1]

In short, we are living in a materialistic culture that fosters and encourages a negative downward cycle toward financial failure. This downward cycle begins with wants and desires (that have been fanned into flame by advertising gimmicks and propaganda) and results in accumulating more and more. Next we find that the things we have accumulated have become obsolete and so we wind up in need, which may be real or imagined (*see* Figure 14).

As one newspaper columnist put it, the famous Alka Seltzer commercial, "I can't believe I ate the whole thing," is really a perfect slogan for our somewhat shamefaced nation. The United States accounts for about one-sixteenth of the earth's population, yet we manage to consume about one-third of the world's energy and half of its resources (while spending $2 billion annually on dieting).[2]

Unfortunately, the bottom line in our consumer society is that many people do wind up in real and dire need, because they have been sucked into spending too much too fast on the wrong things.

The Credit Card Conspiracy

One of the chief contributors to the downward cycle toward financial failure is the hallowed American institution called the credit card. It is just too easy to whip out that piece of plastic and put yourself in overwhelming debt. And while millions of credit card users are warned repeatedly about the high interest rates they are paying, they seem to be blind and deaf to the fact.

One of the most subtle advertising schemes for credit cards that I have seen to date involves a direct mail offer in which you are sent a $1,500 check, accompanied by a masterfully written sales letter that informs you that you can cash the check as a means of applying for your new credit card. The letter creates the impression that the credit card company, out of the goodness of its heart, has put $1,500 in

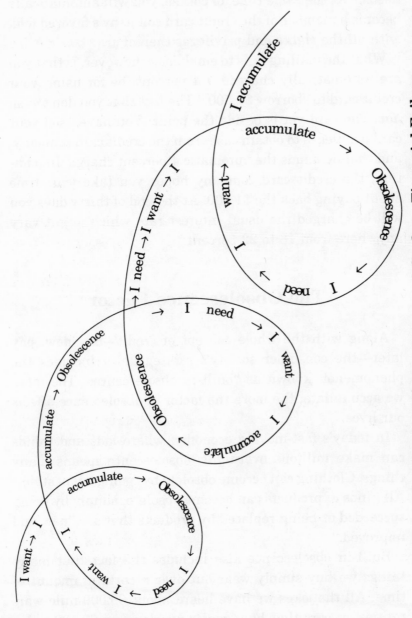

Figure 14: The Negative Downward Cycle to Financial Failure

"instant cash" in your possession to use "according to your needs." At the same time, of course, you will automatically become a member of the credit card company's favored fold, with all the rights and privileges thereof.

What the mailing fails to emphasize, however, is that you are automatically charged a 4 percent fee for using your credit card to "borrow $1,500." The fact that you don't even *have* the card yet is beside the point. You have used your card privileges to obtain cash from the credit card company, and that demands the automatic 4 percent charge. In addition, the credit card company hopes you take your time about paying back the $1,500. At the end of thirty days you will be charged the usual interest rate which might vary anywhere from 18 to 22 percent.

The Obsolescence Factor

Along with the whole concept of credit—buy now, pay later—the consumer society's strategy also includes the phenomenon known as "built-in obsolescence." The more we accumulate, the more the factor of obsolescence affects our lives.

In today's fast-moving economy, where fads and trends can make millions overnight, obsolescence means many things. Clothing can become obsolete by "going out of style." All kinds of products can become obsolete, simply by being succeeded or being replaced by products that are "new and improved."

Built-in obsolescence also includes the fact that many things we buy simply wear out over a certain amount of time. All the jokes we have heard about 60,000-mile warranties on cars that have major problems at 62,100 miles are really not that funny.

It has happened to plenty of people, and it will continue to happen. Despite all of the trumpeting about quality being their major concern, car companies build products to last only so long and calculate that the warranty will run out before the car does.

Recently the "new and improved" strategy lured me into buying another fishing reel. I do a lot of fishing on saltwater, and I thought I was happy with some reels I bought not too long ago, which featured all exterior parts made of graphite or stainless steel, which meant they would never rust, even in saltwater.

But just recently my graphite reels became obsolete. Why? Because "new and better" ones have come on the market equipped with two speeds. One speed allows me to retrieve my casts at a faster pace to attract the fish, then, once I get them hooked, I can switch to a lower speed, which enables me to reel them in with more ease. My old reels had only one speed and sometimes when I got a fish hooked, it was difficult getting him reeled in because the faster gear made it hard to turn the handle as the fish struggled and pulled against the line. With the newer reel, however, I can switch to a lower gear and have the proper ratio to bring the fish to the boat with greater ease.

Granted, I caught plenty of fish with my old reels. I seldom lost a fish because I had only one speed, but, nonetheless, the convenience of the new reel, plus the promises of advertisers that "now you'll never lose that big one," lured me into the store to make the purchase.

The bottom line of the negative cycle concerning finances is that we always seem to wind up feeling more in need than ever. And for millions of people, the needs are real because they have overspent, believing that they had to have certain items, certain pieces of clothing, a certain hairdo, etc., etc., ad infinitum.

Is there a way out of this downward spiral? Of course there is, and it is based on principles that God has built into creation since its very beginning. Will many people take advantage of these principles? Unfortunately, many do not, but on the other hand they are there for you to use, if you're interested in harnessing the power of money.

The Attitude for Financial Success

The positive upward cycle of financial success that I'm about to describe is not designed to help you make a killing on the stock market or get rich quick with a fast real estate deal. What this positive cycle does describe is how being financially responsible can enable anyone to live an abundant, prosperous life.

The positive cycle upward to true financial success (*see* Figure 15) starts with investing (or what the Scripture calls sowing), goes on to developing (or growing your investment), and, finally, to enjoying the results (reap your harvest).

I sometimes call Matthew 7:7 the "lucky verse" of the Bible, a play on words, to be sure, because to believe in God and trust in "luck" is a contradiction in terms. Any financial investment begins with understanding your mission or goal. As Matthew 7:7 says, "Ask, and it will be given to you; seek, and you will find; knock, and it will be opened to you." As God helps you identify your goals, you begin to think in terms of *investing rather than consuming*.

Instead of living for the moment and continually saying, "I've just got to have this or that," you begin setting goals of various kinds, some simple and short-range and others more complex, which may take longer to reach.

What is your purpose in life? What are your dreams, your hopes, your aspirations? In other words, *what is your mission?* What are you really asking God for, what are you seeking and on what door are you truly knocking?

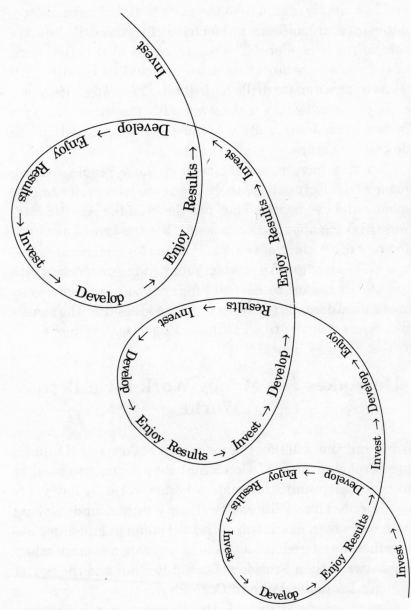

Figure 15: The Positive Upward Cycle of Financial Success

Remember that money is nothing more than a tool that enables you to acquire what you want in life. Money is not an end but simply a means to the ends that you have chosen.

Every year, millions of electric drills and drill bits are sold in America alone. The odd thing about it is that none of the customers buy those drills or drill bits because they want to accumulate drills or drill bits. *They buy a drill or a drill bit because they want a hole.* It's the same way with money—you accumulate it because you want to achieve or do certain things.

You may have heard the saying, "Love people and use money." Unfortunately, there are those who prefer to love money and use people. They are the kind the Apostle Paul was thinking about when he said, "For the love of money is the root of all kinds of evil. . . ."[3] Greed for money can cause you all kinds of grief, but when your driving motivation is to use money to love people, all kinds of good will come: good ideas, good dreams, good hopes, and good results. The money will flow naturally to all of these. I have seen it happen.

He Makes His Money Work for a Better World

For much of his life, the main goal of Armand Hammer, president and CEO of Occidental Petroleum, has been to use his vast wealth to create a better world. A few years ago, Dr. Norman Vincent Peale, my father, and I, along with our wives, had lunch with Dr. Hammer, and as we ate together, he shared his desire to help create a summit meeting between then President Ronald Reagan and the Soviet Union's President Mikhail Gorbachev.

Nearly ninety years old, Dr. Hammer recalled experiences as a youth in Russia, including personal conversations he had with Nicolai Lenin toward the end of Lenin's life. He also told us of conversing with Gorbachev and urging him to create a free market economy that would allow democracy and free enterprise to rule in Russia.

"I told Gorbachev," Dr. Hammer related to us, "that Lenin told me, 'Communism will not work.' "

That summit between Reagan and Gorbachev did take place, of course, and many others have followed between Gorbachev and other American leaders.

In early December 1989, my father was flown on Dr. Hammer's private jet to Moscow, where Dr. Hammer introduced him to Valentin Lazoutkin, deputy director of Gosteleradio, the official government agency overseeing all television broadcasts in the Soviet Union. Right on the spot, my father was given the privilege to preach a brief message, which was taped and later broadcast on December 25 to 200 million Soviet citizens.

In February 1990, my father traveled to the Soviet Union with Dr. Hammer once again to negotiate the taping of another message, which was broadcast over Soviet television on May 27, 1990, the Sunday before Gorbachev's summit meeting with President George Bush.

Subsequent to that, Dr. Hammer also played a part in arranging still more negotiations, during which the Russians agreed to have my father tape ten more messages for broadcast over Soviet television in the fall of 1990.

Because he used his vast wealth and influence at just the right time, Dr. Hammer was a key to opening doors that allowed the Gospel message to be preached nationwide in a land where its open declaration had been forbidden for many decades.

In addition to achieving understanding and world peace between nations, Armand Hammer's other dream is to find a cure for cancer. He has donated $5 million to the Salk Institute for cancer research, and he annually funds the Armand Hammer Cancer Conference at the Salk Institute, which brings together scientists from all over the world to share their work and knowledge.

In a speech given to the National Press Club in Washington, D.C., he said,

> I've been a man of many dreams and I've been fortunate to see many of them come true. But my greatest dream remains to be fulfilled—a lasting peace and a cure for that most dread of diseases, cancer.[4]

Armand Hammer is an outstanding example of what can happen when you use your money to love others.

I Had a Dream But No Money

When I started the Rancho Capistrano Community Church, I had no funds. All I had was a dream and what I believed was a direct call from God. There was no congregation, no group of people among whom we could pass offering plates.

Instead, I had all kinds of needs. I needed to send out mailers to let people know I was starting a church. I needed to put ads in the paper, I needed to contact people, I needed to open an office. I needed a telephone system.

Meeting all of those needs was only a means to my real end—starting a church in southern Orange County, a church that would share the positive message of the grace of Jesus Christ; a church that would help people to achieve healthy self-esteem and healthy self-respect, based on a healthy relationship to God; a church that would help people be free from guilt and open to God's grace; and, above all, a church that would love people.

But how was my dream to come into being? Starting churches takes money, and I had no funds. I decided to ask, seek, and knock. My plan was simple: telephone fifty people and ask each one to give a $500 donation. So I called and I called and I called, and one by one the donations came in. Those "Fifty Founders of Faith" became the financial foundation of my dream—a new church in the San Juan Capistrano area.

If you want to work on resisting the pull of the credit card undertow, start filtering the many wants and desires that consumer society propaganda continually creates by asking yourself two questions:

What is my dream?

What do I believe is the mission God has for me?

I believe that having a mission and a goal that is bigger than you are will keep you from overspending and overindulging in unnecessary luxuries.

How to Manage Your Mission

Step number one in the upward cycle is to find your mission and start investing. Step number two in the cycle is to manage that mission—develop your investment and make it grow.

One of the most powerful scriptural principles I know of regarding money says this: "If you give, you will get! Your gift will return to you in full and overflowing measure, pressed down, shaken together to make room for more, and running over. Whatever measure you use to give—large or small—will be used to measure what is given back to you."[5]

The reason this principle has such power is that it is based on another truth. You see, *we really don't own anything*. Philip Slater observes that, in the distant past

> . . . the land and its products belonged to anyone and
> everyone to use until forcibly expropriated by those
> powerful enough to do so. Most American Indians
> didn't feel they "owned" the land, for example—they
> shared its use with all living beings until they were
> forced off of it.[6]

Slater also has some provocative ideas on the link between ownership and ecology. He goes on to say:

> The environment ultimately belongs to everyone for
> we all share its use, all depend on it for survival, and
> must all cooperate in maintaining it to insure that
> survival. No one can reasonably claim a permanent
> right to a piece of land or water or sky. In the first
> place, no one lives permanently.[7]

Slater is absolutely right. God has created it all, and we
are only stewards of certain parts of His creation for which
we are responsible. Fee simple title to property does not
signify ownership as much as it speaks of my responsibility
to use and manage that property correctly.

I believe that when I purchase something, I am assuming
responsibility for that particular item. I am to treat it
wisely, respectfully, and well. As a good steward and man-
ager, I will seek to make that item a tool to make me a
better person, the world a better place, and ultimately to
glorify the One who provided that item (or the raw material
to make the item) in the first place.

Stopping to think about the responsibilities you are taking on whenever you buy anything is another good way to
avoid a credit card crisis. Owning real estate, for example,
places you under tremendous responsibilities. There are
taxes to pay, and if someone happens to wander onto your
land and get hurt, you may be liable to a lawsuit. In south-

ern Orange County, where San Juan Capistrano is located, there is a law on the books that says if you own a piece of real estate you are required to keep it cleared of weeds and other trash.

The responsibilities of ownership can be enormous, and I believe the only way to meet those responsibilities properly is to develop what you have purchased to its greatest potential. I like to realize that God is investing in me every time He allows me to acquire anything. I am responsible, then, to develop what I've acquired to its greatest potential. In that sense, I give to God and get far more back—blessings pressed down and running over. The more I invest in good stewardship and management, the more God invests in me, and the success cycle continues to turn.

The Team-man-ship Principle

Many people are familiar with the 80–20 principle, which works in many areas of life. In regard to money management, however, I prefer to see it as the 10–80–10 rule: Give the first 10 percent to God, live on 80 percent, invest or save the remaining 10 percent.

To make the 10–80–10 rule work, you have to understand the "team-man-ship principle," which includes spiritual and human aspects. You and God are a team. Your part of the deal is to work as if everything depended on you. Then you count on God for His part and you pray as though everything depended on God.

The best illustration of the team-man-ship principle is a well-known story about a farmer who bought a dilapidated, run-down farm. The fields were full of rocks and weeds, the barns were completely falling apart. Paint was peeling off everything, the fences were down—the whole place was a mess. But the farmer bought it anyway, because it was all he could afford.

The farmer went to work, putting in extra hours clearing the fields, repairing the barns, painting all the buildings, including the farmhouse. Any profits he made were poured back into fixing up the place, and in time his farm became one of the most beautiful in that part of the state.

A new minister was called to the farmer's small church and, according to custom, the new pastor paid a visit on all his members. When he visited the farmer for the first time, he said, "Sir, you have one of the most beautiful farms I have ever seen. The place is absolutely immaculate—it's outstanding."

"Well, thank you very much, Pastor," said the farmer. "I appreciate the compliment."

"You are a very fortunate man," the pastor continued. "God has blessed you very richly by giving you this wonderful farm."

"Oh, I agree with you," replied the farmer. "All that is very true, because of the agreement I have with God. You see, God and I are partners."

"Oh?" the pastor replied, a bit puzzled.

"Oh, yes. God and I are partners. God provided the farm for me, all right, but He really needed some help with managing it. You should have seen it when He had it all by Himself!"

Our team-man-ship with God is based on understanding that there is a twofold side to managing our finances. The human side says we must work as if it all depends on us. The spiritual side says we must pray as if it all depends on God and leave the final results in His hands. When we put these two functions together, we get team-man-ship, which I believe works every time for our success.

The key is to keep the spiritual and human side well balanced. To sit around on your hands and do nothing while asking God to "bless your life" is a sure formula for failure. You can wind up feeling disillusioned and disappointed with God because "He didn't come through." On the other side of the coin, however, you can condition yourself for another kind of failure if you depend entirely on your own efforts and don't include God in your financial picture.

Tithing—A Privilege, Not a Burden

It is ironic that money can be such a touchy subject around the church. I am sure it goes back to what I said earlier about money being a very sacred area of our lives. Nonetheless, Scripture makes it plain about how to find financial success.

"Bring all the tithes into the storehouse . . ." says God, "I will open up the windows of heaven for you and pour out a blessing so great you won't have room enough to take it in!" And then He goes on to say, "Try it! Let me prove it to you! Your crops will be large . . . and all nations will call you blessed, for you will be a land sparkling with happiness. These are the promises of the Lord of Hosts."[8]

Without apology, in fact, with enthusiasm, I urge people to learn the privilege and blessing of tithing—giving God back ten cents out of every dollar He makes it possible for us to earn. After all, where does the money come from in the first place? Who created the heavens and the earth? Who gave you the life that you have today? Who gave you the ability to earn the money that you bring home?

Everything we have is God's, and someday everything will go back to God. As someone once said, you can't take a U-Haul to heaven! I have always liked the story about a wealthy man who died and went to heaven. As he and Saint Peter were walking down the streets of gold, they came to a beautiful mansion, and the man asked, "Ah, is that one mine?"

"No," said Saint Peter, "that's not your home. Follow me; I'll take you to yours."

They walked on and came upon another lovely place, and the rich man said, "Ahh, this must be the one."

"No," said Saint Peter patiently, "this isn't your place either, but just follow me, it isn't far now."

They rounded a bend and came upon a tiny shack. Saint Peter said, "Here is your home."

"What?" said the rich man incredulously. "You mean this is *my* house? *This* is what I will have for all eternity?"

Saint Peter looked at the man for a moment and then simply said, "Well, I did all I could with what you sent."

You see, the whole idea behind giving is that it is like sowing seeds. You reap what you sow. You don't wait to start giving after you've gotten everything else taken care of, the house redecorated, and extra money in your savings account. Start today and, if tithing seems beyond your amount of faith, start somewhere. Commit to give 2 percent, or possibly 5 or 6 percent, and watch what happens.

I believe God offers us a very good arrangement: He gives us 100 percent of what we have and then He says, "Test Me, just put a little faith in Me and see if I will not pour out such a blessing upon you that your storehouses won't be able to handle it."

When you combine the principle of team-man-ship with the principle of giving and do not relent from your commitment, in time *you will see fruit.* As you learn to manage the tithe, you will learn to manage the rest of your finances—what you live on and what you save. Instead of being sucked into the credit card whirlpool, you'll find that you have money to pay the bills and money to invest as well.

By following simple and sound investment policies, you can know blessings beyond your wildest imagination. For example, holding to our 10–80–10 principle, suppose someone earning $20,000 a year puts $2,000 (10 percent of his income) into a bank account at the beginning of each year for forty-one consecutive years. If the money earned only simple (not compound) interest at 10 percent, he would realize $1,051,870 at the end of that time.

Now, I realize this is a highly idealized example but I'm using it to point out the power of interest.

Think of it: Through the power of accumulating interest, in the course of forty-one years, the savings account of only $82,000 will turn into over $1 million! For how the mathematics actually work, see the table below.

How to Become a Millionaire in Forty-one Years

Year			Year		
1	Deposit:	2,000	6	Deposit:	2,000
	Interest:	200		Interest:	1,250
	Total Saved	2,200		Total Saved	15,752
2	Deposit:	2,000	7	Deposit:	2,000
	Interest:	220		Interest:	1,575
	Total Saved	4,420		Total Saved	19,327
3	Deposit:	2,000	8	Deposit:	2,000
	Interest:	442		Interest:	1,932
	Total Saved	6,862		Total Saved	23,259
4	Deposit:	2,000	9	Deposit:	2,000
	Interest:	686		Interest:	2,325
	Total Saved	9,548		Total Saved	27,584
5	Deposit:	2,000	10	Deposit:	2,000
	Interest:	954		Interest:	2,758
	Total Saved	12,502		Total Saved	32,342

Year			Year		
11	Deposit:	2,000	19	Deposit:	2,000
	Interest:	3,234		Interest:	9,219
	Total Saved	37,576		Total Saved	103,414
12	Deposit:	2,000	20	Deposit:	2,000
	Interest:	3,757		Interest:	10,341
	Total Saved	43,333		Total Saved	115,755
13	Deposit:	2,000	21	Deposit:	2,000
	Interest:	4,333		Interest:	11,575
	Total Saved	49,666		Total Saved	139,330
14	Deposit:	2,000	22	Deposit:	2,000
	Interest:	4,966		Interest:	13,933
	Total Saved	56,632		Total Saved	155,263
15	Deposit:	2,000	23	Deposit:	2,000
	Interest:	5,663		Interest:	15,526
	Total Saved	64,295		Total Saved	172,789
16	Deposit:	2,000	24	Deposit:	2,000
	Interest:	6,429		Interest:	17,278
	Total Saved	72,724		Total Saved	192,067
17	Deposit:	2,000	25	Deposit:	2,000
	Interest:	7,272		Interest:	19,206
	Total Saved	81,996		Total Saved	213,273
18	Deposit:	2,000	26	Deposit:	2,000
	Interest:	8,199		Interest:	21,327
	Total Saved	92,195		Total Saved	236,600

Year			Year		
27	Deposit:	2,000	35	Deposit:	2,000
	Interest:	23,660		Interest:	53,004
	Total Saved	262,260		Total Saved	585,045
28	Deposit:	2,000	36	Deposit:	2,000
	Interest:	26,226		Interest:	58,504
	Total Saved	290,486		Total Saved	645,549
29	Deposit:	2,000	37	Deposit:	2,000
	Interest:	29,048		Interest:	64,554
	Total Saved	321,534		Total Saved	712,103
30	Deposit:	2,000	38	Deposit:	2,000
	Interest:	32,153		Interest:	71,210
	Total Saved	355,687		Total Saved	785,313
31	Deposit:	2,000	39	Deposit:	2,000
	Interest:	35,568		Interest:	78,531
	Total Saved	393,255		Total Saved	865,844
32	Deposit:	2,000	40	Deposit:	2,000
	Interest:	39,325		Interest:	86,584
	Total Saved	434,580		Total Saved	954,428
33	Deposit:	2,000	41	Deposit:	2,000
	Interest:	43,458		Interest:	95,442
	Total Saved	480,038		Grand Total	$1,051,870
34	Deposit:	2,000			
	Interest:	48,003			
	Total Saved	530,041			

And, Finally, You Reap the Harvest

Sound management has to lead to good results—to a bountiful harvest. That's why God says that if we give, it will be given back to us—good measure, pressed down, shaken together, and running over.[9] If you'd like to illustrate this principle on your kitchen table, take a box of cereal and pour some into a glass. Then press it down and pack it in tight. Now pour in some more cereal and press it down again. Pour in still more and press that down. Soon, you will have the glass full and overflowing, because there won't be room for one more flake. Those are the kind of results God's Word promises—if you're willing to simply take Him at His Word and trust Him as your Partner.

Many people have money, but they do not have peace. They keep searching for that illusive thing called "happiness." What good is money if it only brings you heartache and pain, or worry and cares? What good is money if you don't have peace in your heart and a smile on your face?

When God helps you manage your money, the peace and the smiles will come. I love the promise given by Jesus Himself: "I am come that you might have life and have it more abundantly."[10]

God's goal for every one of us is to live a life that is full of joy—an abundant life because we know and understand Him and His principles. God loves each one of us. He cares about us and wants to bless us with overflowing blessing. He wants us to use our finances to love people, not the reverse. We are to make all we can, so we can give all we can, and we will see a bountiful harvest as a result.

For financial success, find your mission and set your goals. Discover where you want to invest your life and your efforts. Then move to sound principles of managing your money and your finances. Maybe you need to begin better

Make all you can so you can give all you can.

———⟨——⟩———

money management by cutting up all your credit cards and living more on a cash-only basis.

Try living by the 10–80–10 rule and see what happens. See for yourself what Jesus meant by the "abundant life." Experience the tremendous harvest that only God can provide!

Chapter 8
Success Cycles for
Upward Mobility

I was sitting in the mountain cabin my father and I had built when I got the idea. It was an ambitious idea—and maybe a little crazy to boot. It's my guess that being in that cabin had something to do with it, because building the place had also been ambitious—and a little crazy.

I was in junior high when my father used some inheritance money to buy the lot on which the cabin now stands—actually, *perches* would be a better word. You see, my father chose an "unbuildable lot"—so steep it was almost impossible to get up to a tiny area where we could pour a foundation.

Note that I said *almost impossible*. When people told my father, "You can't build a cabin up there," that only made him more determined. He invited me to join him in his latest adventure in possibility thinking, and we made innumerable weekend trips from our home in Garden Grove, south of Los Angeles, up into the San Bernardino Mountains to an area called Moon Ridge, close to Big Bear Lake.

Rock by rock and brick by brick we built that cabin together. It took us over two years, and by the time it was finished I was fifteen and going to high school.

Our family had gone up to the cabin for the weekend and that's when I got my idea—while sitting there looking out the windows at the beautiful view of Big Bear Lake. Just to my left, I could see some towering mountains, which in the winter become the Gold Mine ski area, still operating today.* I looked out those windows and thought, *Wow, wouldn't it be great to hike to the top of that mountain?*

I knew I couldn't get lost because all I would have to do was go straight uphill. To my teenage eyes, the hike looked like a piece of cake. I probably wouldn't even need to take lunch.

I told my parents about my plan, and the next morning I set out, with zero provisions and nothing with me but the shirt on my back. I estimated that it would be a 4,000-foot climb at most, and, because I was in good shape, I was sure I would be back in short order—probably just in time for a late lunch.

So I started climbing toward the peak—or what I thought was the peak. I finally got to the top, only to discover that ahead of me lay another valley and another peak.

I told myself not to worry. *That's no problem,* I thought. *There is just one more peak to go.* So I climbed down into the valley and up to the top of the next peak, only to learn that another valley and another peak lay ahead of me, and I still wasn't anywhere *near* the top. What I didn't realize was that each peak I was climbing was actually hiding the real peak that was my goal. And so it went on that way, all day long. I would reach a peak only to find another valley and another peak lying ahead.

By late afternoon, I was so sick of seeing peaks I was ready to forget the whole thing, but I stuck with it and

---

* While skiing is still done in this area, it is no longer known as Gold Mine. It is now called Bear Valley.

finally reached the very top, from where I could see across vast valleys on either side. I had arrived at my goal at last.

Footsore, hungry, and tired, I made my way back down the several peaks I had just climbed, and I got back to our cabin just as the sun was setting behind the mountains. You can be sure I ate a hearty dinner that night. I was too young—and too tired—to appreciate the vital principle I had experienced that day. It was a concept that my father would, years later, put into a book, which he entitled *The Peak to Peek Principle*.

In explaining how *peak to peek* works, my father wrote:

> Have you noticed how some people's lives seem to be one success unfolding upon another? Each new achievement appears to upstage the previous one. Every new achievement seems to one-up the last success. That's the incredible way these lives unfold. The base gets bigger and the foundation seems to expand. Their achievement level continues to escalate and climb. How does one explain it?
>
> The question could be raised, "What comes first, achievement followed by a new vision, or a vision followed by achievement?" I believe that the super successful people have discovered a peak experience that gives them a vision of greater things they can accomplish.[1]

By a "peak experience," my father meant some kind of positive event in which you set a goal, reach that goal, and realize you are more than you thought you were. You scale a mountain that might seem small to others, but nonetheless it leaves you able to look upward toward a still higher peak.

That's exactly what I did that day when I climbed peak after peak to the very top of the Gold Mine ski area near Big Bear Lake.

The success cycles I've been describing in this book are built on the peak-to-peek principle. As you reach the top of one peak, you get a peek in your mind's eye at what you can attain the next time around with just a little more effort. As you go from peak to peek you begin to experience power. As my father wrote:

> With each successful experience you will gain inner power to climb higher. Success is a study of the flow of power: how to get it; how to keep it; how to share it; how to restrain it; how to use it; and when.[2]

Remember our definition of success?—"The progressive realization of worthwhile goals." In other words, we never stop setting goals and reaching them. It is important to note that the peak-to-peek principle works best for the wise person who knows his or her limits. We should know what we can accomplish and set obtainable goals. Once having reached those goals, however, from there we can see new horizons, we can begin to dream and envision even greater accomplishments—higher peaks, greater rewards. This is how we gain power to go and grow beyond ourselves, in all areas of life.

We have seen how positive upward cycles of success can overcome negative downward cycles of failure regarding the spiritual, emotional, mental, and physical areas of our lives. In addition, we have applied success cycles to our family, friends, and finances.

In each of these seven areas, we can progressively grow, change, and develop potential we never knew was there. And when we begin to "get on a totally positive roll" in all of these areas at once, success is a constant growing experience. There are no limits on what we can do, what we can become, and what we can accomplish!

There is a verse of Scripture in the New Testament that says it perfectly. When we allow God's power to work within us, He ". . . is able to do far more than we would ever dare to ask or even dream of—infinitely beyond our highest prayers, desires, thoughts, or hopes."[3]

God has given us the challenge to go beyond ourselves, and He has also given us principles for goal setting, as we stretch ourselves to become all that He has in mind for us to be. As we focus on these principles, we develop a "goal mind" that becomes our gold mine. Because I believe goal setting is so important, I want to use this final chapter to look at one more cycle—The Goal Mind Cycle of Success (*see* Figure 16.)

In Everything—Put God First

When I studied philosophy in college, I read the works of Alfred North Whitehead, who said, "The dreams of great dreamers aren't fulfilled, they are always transcended." I believe the Apostle Paul was a great dreamer and a man of vision. One night he had a vision that resulted in the spread of the Gospel from Asia into Europe.[4]

Paul was a living embodiment of the peak-to-peek principle, always pressing toward the highest mark of all—his calling from God.[5]

If any cycle of success is to become a reality, our first goal must be to put God in the forefront of our lives. We must think of Him first, not second or last after we have exhausted all our other resources. If the cycles of success are to work for you, the last thing you ever want to say is, "Well, I guess there's nothing left to do but pray about this." What separates the God-centered person from the one who

A "goal mind" is a gold mine!

———————◆———————

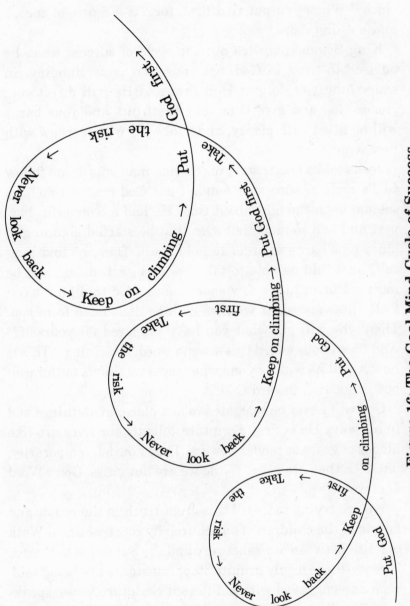

Figure 16: The Goal Mind Cycle of Success

leaves God out is prayer—an opportunity to communicate with Him. When you leave God out, then you have to trust "luck." When you put God first, luck is a figure of speech and nothing more.

King Solomon spelled out the cycle of success when he advised to trust in God, not your own understanding. In everything you do, put Him first and He will direct you. Honor God and give Him your firstfruits and your barns will be filled with plenty, and your vats will overflow with new wine.[6]

Jesus told a tragic story of one rich man who didn't follow God's cycle of success. He didn't put God first—in fact, he seldom even thought about God. He had a wonderful harvest and had so much left over that he started planning to build new barns in order to hold it all. Then, he told himself, he would be able to take his ease, eat, drink, and be merry. But in just a few short hours, God told him, "You fool! This very night your life will be demanded from you. Then who will get what you have prepared for yourself?" And then Jesus added this solemn word of warning: "This is how it will be with anyone who stores up things for himself but is not rich toward God."[7]

God will never be relegated to last place. In all things and in all ways He is first. Scripture tells us our lives are like blades of grass or tender flowers. They flourish temporarily, but then they are gone. While we are but grass, God's Word is eternal.

We are trying to instill this great truth in the minds and hearts of the children of our church by constructing a Walk of Faith between our sanctuary and the Sunday school area. Twenty-three lovely granite stepping-stones are being laid, each one engraved with a different Scripture verse, speaking of God's everlasting promises and power. Following is just a sampling of the power-laden thoughts upon which you would trod if you ever took our Walk of Faith:

172

WITHOUT FAITH, SUCCESS IS IMPOSSIBLE[8]

I CAN DO EVERYTHING THROUGH GOD WHO GIVES ME STRENGTH[9]

ALL THINGS WORK TOGETHER FOR GOOD TO THOSE WHO LOVE GOD[10]

GOD WHO BEGAN A GOOD WORK IN YOU WILL CARRY IT ON TO COMPLETION[11]

Members of our congregation have been invited to purchase one of the steps—in memory of loved ones or simply as a gesture of love and support. When finished, the Walk of Faith will be a beautiful area. It is already landscaped with a waterfall, flowers, and other plants. All that remains is the installation of a few more of the stepping-stones containing God's powerful promises.

The real purpose of the Walk, however, is not decorative, but practical and educational. As our children use these stepping-stones while going to Sunday school class, they will read the verses, and powerful principles and ideas will be engraved on their subconscious minds. While moving back and forth between church and Sunday school, they will be continually reminded of the powerful ideas that can keep them on positive upward success cycles all of their lives.

When you realize that God is first, everything else falls into place. Success begins to happen. The wheels of success continue to turn and you can move on, from peak to peek.

Prayer is no longer a chore; it is an exciting means of communicating with God and gaining His guidance. And it is only through God's guidance that we end up where God wants us to be. Human beings are not designed to be like water, which always flows to the lowest spot. A human being is designed to be like the salmon, or the eagle, and when we put God first, He helps us rise to greater heights. One of my favorite poems says it so well:

High Flight

Oh, I have slipped the surly bonds of earth
And danced the skies on laughter-silvered wings;
Sunward I've climbed, and joined the tumbling mirth
Of sun-split clouds—and done a hundred things
You have not dreamed of—wheeled and soared and swung
High in the sunlit silence. Hov'ring there,
I've chased the shouting wind along, and flung
My eager craft through footless halls of air.
Up, up the long, delirious, burning blue
I've topped the windswept heights with easy grace
Where never lark, or even eagle flew.
And, while with silent, lifting mind I've trod
The high untrespassed sanctity of space,
Put out my hand, and touched the face of God.

JOHN GILLESPIE MAGEE, JR.

Step Out in Faith—and Risk

When you realize that God is first, everything else falls into place. You have the faith—and the courage—to move on and to take risks. You try that first peak, then you get a peek at the next, and you are willing to try that one as well.

Climbing peaks is not easy. God never intended that it should be. I like the way Oswald Chambers puts it:

There are times in the life of every disciple when things are not clear or easy, when it is not possible to know what to do or to say. Such times of darkness come as a discipline to the character and as a means to a fuller knowledge of the Lord. Such darkness is a time for listening, for speaking. The Lord shares the darkness with His disciples. He is there.[12]

Granted, when you begin taking steps of faith—risking— the success is not always certain. In fact, you may have moments when failure can loom before you like a mountain. We have climbed many peaks ourselves in the first years of building a new church in Orange County. One of those peaks has been assembling an outstanding staff to minister to the needs of our congregation.

Currently, our full-time staff consists of myself and my secretary, Carol Neidhardt. Working part-time for us are Nate Morrison, minister of pastoral care; Lynn Taylor, who directs our Christian education area as director of Christian development; Sheldon Disrud, our choir director; and Kathy Harris, our organist.

In addition, Chris Knippers is a licensed psychologist who, while not a member of our church staff, uses our facilities for his counseling ministry. He also offers his services to the church to give leadership training and assistance to our support groups.

Every time we have added a staff member, it has been an important step of faith—a risk, if you please. But God has honored every appointment and our ministry continues to grow.

Dr. Peale Comes to Rancho Capistrano

Not long ago we stepped out in faith and invited Norman Vincent Peale to speak at our church. Now, this might sound simple enough, especially when a man of Norman Vincent Peale's stature offers to speak for nothing! But, in truth, having Dr. Peale come meant spending thousands of dollars for mailings, advertising, and renting chairs and a podium for an outdoor setting.

Our sanctuary holds four hundred people, but anticipating that God would bring far more listeners than that, we decided to hold this particular service outdoors. It was a beautiful summer day and thirteen hundred people came to hear one of America's greatest teachers of possibility thinking.

That morning Dr. Peale helped all of us deal with one of the most common of all human problems—self-doubt. Throughout his career, Dr. Peale has specialized in ministering to people who do not actually believe they can. They put themselves down constantly, if not by word at least in their thoughts. They just think they can't do it because they have such a low opinion of themselves.

One illustration he told that day remains forever fixed in my mind. Dr. Peale mentioned a trip that he made to Hong Kong, and he described walking through the twisted little streets of Kowloon where literally millions of people shopped for every kind of merchandise under the sun. Dr. Peale stopped before one of these small shops and read a sign that said, "Tattoo Studio." In the window were samples of all the various designs and pictures that customers could have tattooed on their bodies—beautiful girls, mermaids, flags, or various slogans, one of which was "BORN TO LOSE."

His curiosity fully aroused, Dr. Peale went into the studio and said to the Chinese proprietor: "That one . . . BORN TO LOSE. . . ."

"Take off your jacket," said the tattoo artist, assuming Dr. Peale was a customer.

"No," responded Dr. Peale. "I don't want that tattooed on me, but I want to ask you a question. Does anybody in his right mind ever come into this studio and actually have tattooed into his quivering flesh the awful statement, 'BORN TO LOSE'?"

"Yes," answered the proprietor, "a few."

Incredulously, Dr. Peale asked, "But why would anybody do that?"

The old tattoo artist looked at Dr. Peale and said simply, "Before tattoo on body, tattoo in mind."

How true! Before anybody could put BORN TO LOSE on your arm, or anywhere else on your body, you would have to tell yourself over a long period of time that you are, indeed, a born loser.

Another point Dr. Peale shared that morning was what he calls "The Think Principle." Thomas A. Edison said, "The only reason we have the body is to carry the brain around." That's an extreme way of pointing out just how important our minds really are. In the mind we think, create, envision, and remember. The mind is where we have faith. As we saw in chapters 2 and 3, we are what our minds produce.

If we hit problems, pain, and tragedy and respond negatively, our problems, pain, and tragedy will only be increased. If we can react to problems, pain, and tragedy with positive, faith-filled thinking, there is no problem that can ultimately defeat us. And there is no goal or dream we cannot achieve.

Set Your Goal and Don't Look Back

On the day I was ordained, September 21, 1981, my father gave me a necklace with a medallion. On one side was the inscription, "To my son, Robert Anthony Schuller, on your ordination to the Gospel ministry, from your father, Reverend Robert H. Schuller."

Engraved on the other side of the medallion are three

Scripture references, including Jesus' challenge: "No one, having put his hand to the plow, and looking back, is fit for the kingdom of God."[13] As He often did, Jesus used an image of an everyday occurrence to help His followers grasp the truth. If they decided to follow Him, they couldn't look back. They had to keep their eyes straight ahead or face all kinds of problems.

Many Third World farmers of today plow the same way farmers did in biblical Palestine. It takes a tremendous amount of effort to keep the light wooden plow digging deep and straight. Once you put your hand to the plow, it is totally unacceptable to ever look back. If you do, two things can happen: (1) Your oxen can wander off course and your furrow can become crooked. (2) You take your weight off the plow, which keeps it from making a deep enough furrow in the earth.

Not looking back after putting one's hand to the plow was such a key principle that even today in many parts of the Middle East while traveling or working, to look back is considered a sure way to bring ultimate misfortune upon yourself.[14] The point Jesus made is clear: He asks us for total commitment. He wants us to put all our strength into serving God, always looking ahead, never back. We are to look at what lies before us, not at past failures or mistakes.

Failure Is a Bend, Not an End

In every area of life we have looked at, there is a negative failure cycle and a positive success cycle. If you dwell on your mistakes or misfortunes, you will spiral downward in a continuing cycle of failure. But if you learn to roll with life's punches, you can turn things around and begin to succeed.

The principle of "rolling with the punches" was graphically demonstrated to me when I was in college and made the varsity wrestling team as a freshman. Naturally, I thought I was pretty good—until the day I challenged a small, slightly built Korean who lived in my dorm. He was a bit older than the rest of us, and we seldom saw much of him because he kept to himself. On one occasion, however, he came up as another member of the wrestling team and I were discussing our sport and boasting about how it was the finest of all the arts of self-defense.

Yes, a boxer might get in a couple of punches, but then we would put him in a hold, throw him to the ground, and that would be it. Then we started talking about karate and how our wrestling skills would still be superior to any karate punches that might be thrown. Our Korean friend listened for a while and then said, "I disagree with you."

"You disagree with us?" I said incredulously.

"Yes, I disagree with you."

"Well," I responded, "I bet I can put you down and keep you down."

The Korean accepted my challenge on the spot, and we went out in the carpeted hallway to prove who was better.

I got down into my traditional wrestling stance to take my shot—and I made it a good one because I wanted to prove to this guy that I knew what I was talking about. I dipped down and put him in a fireman's carriage, but as soon as I lifted him up, he rolled over, and all of sudden I found myself landing on my back while he was on his feet.

Dumbfounded, I got to my feet and took another shot. But this time he moved about one step to the left, and I went flying over his leg and landed on my back again, while he was still on his feet.

He toyed with me for a while longer, and then let us know that he was trained in judo, which is based on the principle of using an opponent's size and strength to your own advantage. Whenever I came at him, he would simply go with the motion and use my momentum to throw me. In other words, he knew how to roll with the punches.

I never forgot my Korean friend and what he taught me that day. Besides a good dose of humility, I also received a principle for living. When you suffer failure or frustration in trying to reach a goal, roll with the force of the blow, try a different route.

One of my favorite poems says it this way:

The Zigzag Path

We climbed the height by the zigzag path
  And wondered why—until
We understood it was made zigzag
  To break the force of the hill.

A road straight up would prove too steep
  For the traveler's feet to tread;
The thought was kind in its wise design
  Of a zigzag path instead.

It is often so in our daily life;
  We fail to understand
That the twisting way our feet must tread
  By love alone was planned.

Then murmur not at the winding way,
  It is our Father's will
To lead us Home by the zigzag path,
  To break the force of the hill.[15]

AUTHOR UNKNOWN

This bit of verse helps me to understand why God allows us to fail from time to time. He knows we need to follow a zigzag path, not only to break the force of the hill we are climbing, but to experience the necessary troubles and tests that will make us stronger, better people. One of the great followers of the zigzag path was the inventor Thomas Edison. Some members of his staff once came to him and asked why they had failed in a particular experiment. Edison replied, "What do you mean, you have failed?"

"Well, we have tried this experiment seven hundred times and we still haven't cracked the answer. We've failed."

"You haven't failed," responded Edison. "You just know seven hundred reasons why it won't work."

Edison and his fellow workers always went on to find the solution—what *would* work, and that is the key. Failure is not the end of the road; it is the bend in the road. The difference between winners and losers is how they respond to failure. The last man to bat .400 in the major leagues was Ted Williams. As good as the "Splendid Splinter" was, he still failed six out of every ten times he went to bat. What made him the greatest hitter in baseball history was his response to his failures. He always came back to the plate knowing that "this time" he'd get a base hit, and he often did.

Paul Tournier has observed, "God's plan is fulfilled, not just in the obedience of inspired men, but also through their error." If Ted Williams had considered every strikeout or pop-up to be a disaster from which he could not recover, he wouldn't have become the great hitter that he was.

When you suffer a setback, because of your own mistakes or possibly someone else's, you have a choice. You can allow that setback to put you on a negative downward cycle or you can realize that God uses our failures and mistakes to strengthen us. He allows difficulties to make us better people and show us there is another way.

Envision What You and God Can Do

The second Scripture reference on that medallion my father gave me is one of the greatest promises the Apostle

Paul ever penned: "Being confident of this very thing, that He who has begun a good work in you will complete it. . . ."[16] While Paul was referring ultimately to the final destiny of everyone who believes in Christ, I believe these words also apply to any work that we undertake—any goal that we set, any peak that we want to climb in life. Indeed, our entire life is a series of peaks and valleys, which result in reaching a final summit—eternal fellowship with God Himself.

Whatever peak we choose to climb because we've put God first, we can be assured that He will help us carry our task to completion. He doesn't lead us down the primrose path only to abandon us at some crucial point along the way. He loves us far too much for that.

The late E. Stanley Jones, who over the years was one of my mentors, once said, "Faith is not jumping to conclusions, it's concluding to jump." Once you make that conclusion to jump, once you set your hands to the plow and put your eye upon your goal, then accept the goal and dream and desire that God has given to you, and never look back. Never take your eyes off your dream.

In chapter 2, I mentioned how my sister, Carol, horribly injured in a motorcycle accident, focused on solving her problem and regained her health. In her case, Carol focused on seeing her white cells marching into battle against her life-threatening infections and winning. Related closely to this kind of positive focusing is another concept called *dynamic imaging,* developed by Dr. Norman Vincent Peale. In describing how dynamic imaging works, Dr. Peale says:

> It consists of vividly picturing, in your conscious mind, a desired goal or objective and holding that image until it sinks into your unconscious mind, where it releases great, untapped energies. It works best when it is combined with a strong religious

faith, backed by prayer, and the seemingly illogical technique of giving thanks for benefits before they are received. When the imaging concept is applied steadily and systematically, it solves problems, strengthens personalities, improves health, and greatly enhances the chances for success in any kind of endeavor.[17]

Dynamic imaging is nothing more than using your imagination, a God-given gift, to see yourself accomplishing the goals you have set, acquiring what you need to acquire in order to reach those goals, and becoming everything that God wants you to be.

There is a lot of confusion about a concept like dynamic or positive imaging. Whenever someone comes up with a good idea, other people will come along and want to carry it too far or use it incorrectly. Suppose, for example, a woman decides she will become a butterfly by using positive imaging. She spends the entire day dreaming about being a butterfly and repeating over and over, "I am a butterfly . . . I am a butterfly . . . I am a butterfly."

Twenty times a minute for twenty-four hours she repeats, "I am a butterfly," and at the end of that twenty-four hours is she a butterfly? No, she is hoarse.

Positive imaging works only when you do. I could have told myself, "You are a great mountain climber," twenty times a minute for twenty-four hours, but I would have been no closer to the top of that Gold Mine peak. The point was, I had to get out and start climbing.

The Secret of Success—WORK!

Donald Kendle, chairman of the board and chief executive officer of the Pepsi Cola Corporation, was asked why it is that some people rise to the top. His response, "There is no place where success comes before work, except in the dictionary."

A few years ago a member of our congregation became a consummate example of possibility thinking and dynamic imaging. When I first met Kerry Titello, I did not even begin to anticipate his faith, determination, and fortitude. He had a dream that had become his life goal. That goal was to be a pilot for a major airline.

Kerry had just come out of the armed forces where he had been trained as a helicopter pilot. Unfortunately, he had zero experience in flying jet aircraft.

When Kerry told me what he wanted to do, I have to admit my heart sank a little for him. Because my wife, Donna, had been a flight attendant for Continental Airlines, she knew something about their bankruptcy problems. They had laid off hundreds of pilots with literally thousands of hours of flight time. All of these pilots were out there looking for jobs and here was a man who didn't even qualify as a rookie jet pilot because he'd never even trained for the task. With zero hours of experience in flying jet aircraft, Kerry Titello was telling me he was going to get a job flying for a major airline!

It wouldn't happen—it couldn't happen—and I knew it. But here I was, his pastor, the one who had been telling him to dream dreams, have goals, and do positive imaging through his faith in God. What was I supposed to say? Perhaps I could tell him, "I'll bet you would make a great commercial helicopter pilot. There is a tremendous demand for them these days, you know."

I chose to tell Kerry that becoming a pilot for an airline would be difficult, but that he should go for it. Then he told me his second dream. A bachelor, he had decided that he was going to get married. He wanted to find the right woman and marry her. I was more enthusiastic about encouraging him along those lines. His chances of finding a woman to marry seemed a lot better to me than his chances of finding a job flying for a major airline like United or American!

Kerry pursued his two dreams, especially his goal to work for a major airline. Slowly he made progress, first taking a job with a commuter outfit and then doing air-taxi work during the 1984 Summer Olympics, shuttling VIPs between the various events.

He kept filling out applications to work for major airlines and kept getting turned down. He spent almost all his money on getting more training but still there was no breakthrough.

Then in March 1986, he successfully went through the most rigorous series of physical and mental exams and screenings I had ever heard of. There is much more to Kerry's story, which I tell in more detail in another book.[18] The point is, Kerry Titello had a dream and he never took his eyes off his goal. Did he ever get married? Oh, yes, right after completing flight school for American Airlines in Dallas, Texas. Today he flies regularly for American all over the nation.

Faith Knocks the *'T* Off *CAN'T*

When you put your hand to the plow, never look back. Always be confident that when God begins a good work in you, He will complete it. Above all, be faithful. A third passage of Scripture on that medallion my father gave me promises: ". . . Be faithful until death, and I will give you the crown of life."[19]

Those words describe the great paradox of faith. We are to be faithful until the end, and then we die. But in dying we live. We reach the final peak of success. Success is never final in this life because success is not a place we can reach, it is a journey.

Success is the ever-progressive realization of worthwhile goals. Success is the peak-to-peek principle in action. We climb to the top of a peak, and from there we can peek at another pinnacle. We see greater peaks, greater mountains, and greater possibilities with new strength and new vitality.

With new vigor and self-confidence, we dream new dreams and see even greater visions. We recognize new goals that God has set for us and we begin to climb again, knowing that He is at work within us, giving us the will and the desire to succeed.

The difference between failure cycles and success cycles is the difference between thinking you *can't* and thinking you *can*. When Dr. Norman Vincent Peale spoke at Rancho Capistrano, he closed his message with a story about a teacher he had in the fifth grade—George Reeves. Standing six-foot-three and weighing at least 220 pounds, he always wore a long, dignified coat. In those days, he was called Professor Reeves, even though he taught fifth graders.

Professor Reeves had a habit of suddenly thundering for no apparent reason, "SILENCE!" And when Professor Reeves demanded silence, he got silence from everyone. Then he would get up, take a piece of chalk, and write on the blackboard in giant letters the word *CAN'T*.

Dusting off his fingers, he would look back at young Norman Peale and all of his classmates and ask, "What do I do now?"

Because the class had seen him do this many times before, they knew exactly the answer he wanted.

"Knock the *T* off the *CAN'T*," they would all chorus.

With a sweeping gesture and coattails flying, Professor Reeves would erase the *'T* and then turn around and say, triumphantly, "Young ladies and gentlemen [he never called them boys and girls], let that be a lesson to you and never forget it. You can if you think you can with the help of Jesus Christ, your Lord and Savior."

Yes, this was in a *public* school, and I suppose George Reeves's remarks would be "illegal" today. But the professor didn't worry about that. He was interested in telling young people the truth about themselves—that they were endowed with power from on high *when they believed*.

If George Reeves were with us today, he would tell us the same thing. When you believe, when you think you can with Christ, *you will succeed!*

Source Notes

Introduction—There's Got to Be More to Life Than This!

1. John 10:10.

Chapter 1: Faith Gets the Wheels Turning

1. Isaiah 40:31.
2. Matthew 7:7.
3. Psalm 37:3–5.
4. Matthew 7:9–11.
5. James 4:10.
6. Philippians 4:13.
7. Mark 10:27.
8. Philippians 4:13.
9. Hebrews 11:1.

Chapter 2: As You Think, You Will Be

1. Nan Silver, "Do Optimists Live Longer?" *American Health*, November 1986, p. 50.
2. Ibid.
3. Ibid., p. 53.
4. Denis Waitley, *Being the Best* (Nashville: Thomas Nelson Publishers, 1987), p. 154.
5. Ibid., p. 155.
6. Proverbs 16:20 TLB.
7. Mark Fineman, "Philippine Killer Does His Penance Yearly on a Cross," *Los Angeles Times*, Saturday, April 2, 1988, p. 4, Part 1.

8. Robert A. Schuller, *Getting Through the Going-Through Stage* (Nashville: Thomas Nelson Publishers, 1986); Robert A. Schuller, *Power to Grow Beyond Yourself* (Old Tappan, N.J.: Fleming H. Revell Company, 1987).
9. Ray A. Kroc, *Grinding It Out* (New York: Berkeley Books, 1978), p. 201.
10. Philippians 2:12, 13 AT.

Chapter 3: Manage Your Moods or They'll Manage You

1. David D. Burns, *Feeling Good* (New York: New American Library, 1980), p. 9.
2. Ibid., p. 11.
3. Romans 8:28.
4. In the Jewish Scriptures, the Torah consists of the Pentateuch, the Books of Genesis, Exodus, Leviticus, Numbers, and Deuteronomy.
5. Ben Patterson, *Waiting* (Downers Grove, Ill.: InterVarsity Press, 1989), p. 57.
6. John 15:9–11.
7. Harold Kushner, *When All You've Ever Wanted Isn't Enough* (New York: Summit Books, 1986), p. 25.
8. Ibid., pp. 22, 23.
9. John 15:9–12 NIV.
10. Philippians 1:4 NIV.

Chapter 4: You Are What You Eat—And Then Some

1. John Comereski, MAT affiliations, American College of Sports Medicine, Weider Research Group, "Sports Fitness Hotline," *Muscle & Fitness Magazine*, June 1989, p. 33.
2. See especially Kenneth H. Cooper, *Aerobics* (New York: Bantam Books, 1968); Kenneth H. Cooper, *The New Aerobics* (New York: Bantam Books, 1970); Kenneth H. Cooper, *The Aerobics Program for Total Well-Being* (New York: M. Evans and Company, Inc., 1982).
3. *Muscle & Fitness Magazine*, April 1989, p. 29.
4. 1 Timothy 4:8 PHILLIPS.
5. Genesis 6:3.
6. From the Office of the Actuary, Social Security Administration, Reported in *Newsweek*, March 5, 1990, p. 46.
7. Udo Erasmus, *Fats and Oils* (Vancouver, B.C.: Alive Books, 1989), p. 315.
8. Ibid.
9. 1 Corinthians 10:31; 6:19.
10. Kenneth H. Cooper, *The Aerobics Program for Total Well-Being* (New York: M. Evans and Company, Inc., 1982), p. 39.
11. Barbara Kantrowitz, "A Heavyweight Fuss Over the New Fake Fats," *Newsweek*, March 5, 1990. p. 41.
12. Rosa Salter, "It's Easy to Work Fitness in Without Working Out," *Los Angeles Times*, July 10, 1990, p. E3.
13. Patricia Ormsby Borer, *Twenty % Fat ... What's That?* (Rancho Santa Fe, Calif.: Vitaerobics, 1987), p. 10.

14. The estimates of 1,500 calories per day to maintain weight for women and 2,200 calories per day to maintain weight for men vary somewhat with age. For examples of how these figures can range up and down, see Dr. Kenneth H. Cooper, *The Aerobics Program for Total Well-Being* (New York: M. Evans and Company, Inc., 1982), p. 43.
15. Dr. Robert Haas, *Eat to Succeed* (New York: The New American Library, 1987). For Dr. Haas's food composition tables, see pp. 249–314.
16. Dr. Robert Haas, *Eat to Win* (New York: New American Library, 1985). For Dr. Haas's "Eat to Win" recipe section, see pp. 231–326.
17. Galatians 6:8.
18. Kenneth H. Cooper, *The Aerobics Program for Total Well-Being*, p. 125.
19. Covert Bailey, *Fit or Fat?* (Boston: Houghton Mifflin Company, 1977), p. 34.

Chapter 5: Your Home—A Haven of Peace?

1. Isaiah 40:31.
2. Matthew 9:2.
3. Matthew 14:27.
4. John S. Lang, "How Genes Shape Personality," *U.S. News & World Report*, April 13, 1987, p. 58.
5. Ibid., p. 58.
6. Matthew 18:21, 22.
7. Hebrews 12:11 NIV.
8. Gary Smalley and John Trent, *The Blessing* (Nashville: Thomas Nelson Publishers, 1986), p. 9.
9. Psalm 17:8.
10. Matthew 9:20; 14:35, 36.
11. Luke 6:19.
12. Mark 10:14.
13. Isaiah 55:11, 12 AT.

Chapter 6: Building Your Network of Friends

1. Charles Durham, *When You're Feeling Lonely* (Downers Grove, Ill.: InterVarsity Press, 1984), p. 16.
2. Ibid.
3. Genesis 2:18.
4. John 13:34.
5. Precise details on the story of Telemachus have been lost in antiquity. One account (William Barclay, *The Gospel of Matthew*, Vol. 2, Edinburgh: The St. Andrew Press, 1957, p. 86) reports that Telemachus was run through by one of the gladiators when he would not let the fighting go on. Another account (Kenneth Scott Latourette, *A History of the Expansion of Christianity*, Vol. 1, San Francisco: Harper and Row Publishers, 1937, p. 245) reports that Telemachus was stoned to death by a mob of nominal Christians because he "spoiled their fun." I chose Barclay's version and embellished the story in certain areas for additional impact. Whatever happened that day in the arena, Telemachus did make many friends, because he

loved other people and wanted them to realize how important they were in God's sight.

Chapter 7: Harnessing the Power of Money

1. Philip Slater, *The Pursuit of Loneliness* (Boston: Beacon Press, 1970), p. 28.
2. David B. Wilson, "No Slogans; Let's All Fast," *Boston Globe*, September 14, 1974. Quoted by Philip Slater in *The Pursuit of Loneliness*, p. 29.
3. 1 Timothy 6:10.
4. John Bryson, *The World of Armand Hammer* (New York: Harry N. Abrams, Inc., Publishers, 1985), p. 152.
5. Luke 6:38 TLB.
6. Philip Slater, *The Pursuit of Loneliness*, p. 178.
7. Ibid., p. 179.
8. Malachi 3:10–12 TLB.
9. Luke 6:38.
10. John 10:10 AT.

Chapter 8: Success Cycles for Upward Mobility

1. Robert H. Schuller, *The Peak to Peek Principle* (Garden City, N.Y.: Doubleday and Company, Inc., 1980), p. 5.
2. Ibid., pp. 3, 4.
3. Ephesians 3:20 TLB.
4. Acts 16:6–10.
5. Philippians 3:12–14.
6. Proverbs 3:5–10.
7. Luke 12:16–21 NIV.
8. Hebrews 11:1 AT.
9. Philippians 4:13 AT.
10. Romans 8:28.
11. Philippians 1:6 AT.
12. Oswald Chambers, *My Utmost for His Highest* (New York: Dodd, Mead Company, 1935).
13. Luke 9:62.
14. See "Never Look Back," Commentary by Paul David Dunn, *The New King James Version* (Nashville: Thomas Nelson Publishers, 1984), p. 1111.
15. *Parables, Etc.* April 1986, Saratoga Press, P.O. Box 8, Plattville, Col. 80651.
16. Philippians 1:6.
17. Norman Vincent Peale, *Dynamic Imaging* (Old Tappan, N.J.: Fleming H. Revell Company, 1982), p. 13.
18. Robert A. Schuller, *The World's Greatest Comebacks* (Nashville: Thomas Nelson Publishers, 1988), pp. 199–201.
19. Revelation 2:10.